WOMEN VS ANGER

ANGER MANAGEMENT FOR WOMEN : TAKE CONTROL OF YOUR EMOTIONS, MAINTAIN HEALTHY ANGER, AND RESTORE YOUR PEACE OF MIND

YASMIN A.

© **Copyright Yasmin A. 2021 - All rights reserved.**

The content contained within this book may not be reproduced, duplicated, or transmitted without direct written permission from the author or the publisher.

Under no circumstances will any blame or legal responsibility be held against the publisher, or author, for any damages, reparation, or monetary loss due to the information contained within this book. Either directly or indirectly. You are responsible for your own choices, actions, and results.

Legal Notice:

This book is copyright protected. This book is only for personal use. You cannot amend, distribute, sell, use, quote, or paraphrase any part, or the content within this book, without the consent of the author or publisher.

Disclaimer Notice:

Please note the information contained within this document is for educational and entertainment purposes only. All effort has been executed to present accurate, up to date, and reliable, complete information. No warranties of any kind are declared or implied. Readers acknowledge that the author is not engaging in the rendering of legal, financial, medical, or professional advice. The content within this book has been derived from various sources. Please consult a licensed professional before attempting any techniques outlined in this book.

By reading this document, the reader agrees that under no circumstances is the author responsible for any losses, direct or indirect, which are incurred as a result of the use of the information contained within this document, including, but not limited to, — errors, omissions, or inaccuracies.

CONTENTS

Introduction   v

1. What Is Anger?   1
2. How Can I Become Better at Managing My Anger?   13
3. Anger and the Gender Differences   28
4. Is There Such a Thing as Healthy Anger?   39
5. An In-Depth Look at Trauma and the Relationship with Anger   45
6. Child to Parent Violence   63
7. Anger and Our Physical Health   84
8. Train Your Brain to Change the Outcomes   96
9. Learning To Forgive and Seeking Forgiveness   108
10. Be Compassionate To Yourself   121

Conclusion   135
References   141

INTRODUCTION

My aunt is my idol. She is wise, caring, and so open you can talk to her about anything. But boy doesn't she have a temper. Just last family wedding, her granddaughter's juice bottle was thrown at her husband as he asked if he could have a cup of tea as we frantically started serving the evening meal for all the guests. The family joke is that it's lucky that she has such a terrible aim.

The reason we can love my aunt is that it is often my uncle that pushes her buttons for a reaction. It's how their relationship works, and I admire them for this. They laugh and joke, he goes too far, she throws something, and they kiss and make up. When I asked my aunt and uncle how they have remained so happy, they both said that they never go to bed angry.

INTRODUCTION

My other influential experience with anger was not so healthy. My father had anger issues. When people ask if I take after my mom or my dad, I only say that I look like my mom, because deep down it hurts to admit that I have the same angry streak as my dad.

Though both of these family members have a temper, the consequences of both are far from comparable.

There is not a single person in the world who doesn't feel angry at some point in their life. The stresses and strains of today's world push us to unimaginable limits. It is rare that we can leave our 9 to 5 jobs without taking responsibilities home. Our free time is taken up by activities we have to do rather than what we want to do. Our children are obsessed with technology and it is hard to get more than a grunt from them. One situation roles into the next and emotions start to boil.

People get angry with us and we can feel angry. We can get angry because the queue in the supermarket is taking too long or because a certain politician did something stupid. These moments of anger rise and fall, and we can continue with our lives as normal. But when the queue in the supermarket becomes part of the daily routine or your boss continues to ask too much of you, anger isn't just an emotion, it becomes part of who you are.

INTRODUCTION

You wake up in the morning and you are angry, you go to bed and you are angry. Your husband is angry, your kids are angry, and your colleagues are angry. There is no beauty or peace in the world. This takes its toll. Before we know it, our moments of frustration have turned to aggressive outbursts which lead us to feel terrible about ourselves. Anxiety and depression are just around the corner. Some people are aware of the slippery slope, others only realize when they are caught in the vicious cycle. Both are extremely challenging to overcome.

If you are like me, you will have people in your life that want to help you. These loved ones will tell you that you need to control your temper or let go of your anger. Unfortunately, at the time, this only made me angrier. Identifying the problem might not be the challenge. Understanding how to deal with it is. With so much weight on our shoulders the pressure to find a solution to manage our anger needs to have almost instant results but at the same time, it has to be thorough enough so that it doesn't feel like a band-aid on a broken bone.

I lost my dad, my sister-in-law and one of my sisters, in the space of a month. My children were all at different stages of puberty and it was as if all three were working hard to infuriate me. I took it out on my friends, my family, and my

INTRODUCTION

colleagues, who understandably began to struggle with the constant negative attitude in the household and the office. It wasn't even like we were walking on eggshells; we were all tiptoeing through a minefield.

The knock-on-effects at work were also apparent. I couldn't cope with even the smallest mistakes my team members were making. My superiors questioned if I was ok and my response was always through gritted teeth. Their patience with me was starting to wear thin. I knew that my job was at risk because of my temper but I still couldn't find a way to control myself.

Regardless of whether you are a parent or not, you can imagine the dagger that goes straight through your heart when your child says they hate you. What hurt, even more, was the fear in my child's eyes as they waited for me to burst into anger. I knew at this point that if I wanted to keep my family and my job, I had to make a change and I needed help.

I had never been keen on self-help books (which I know is ironic) nor therapy but I also appreciated that I could learn from both. I knew that therapy would help me to unravel the depressive state I found myself in. I also decided that my own education would enable me to focus more on the problems that women have to deal with and the particular problems I was facing as a mum with a career.

INTRODUCTION

The combination of professional help and a passion for self-improvement led to massive changes in a surprisingly short period of time. I learnt so much about myself, naturally, some of which came from my childhood but just as much came from my years of being an adult. Rather than focusing too much on the source, I became hungry to discover what could be done to ease the pain I was feeling in the present. I practiced different techniques, some of which worked and others that didn't. Bit by bit I chipped away at the anger that my loved ones only saw, and I learnt how to free myself from the years of pain I had been suffering with. Finally, I began to feel happier, and I was able to enjoy life as it was meant to be enjoyed.

This is what has led me to where we are today. I am so grateful for my experiences and all that I have learnt. I am lucky that I managed to gain control over my anger before it completely destroyed my life. While discovering how to become a better person and manage my emotions, I was able to see the difference between healthy anger, like my aunt, and unhealthy anger, like my dad.

I have dealt with anger from all angles and all perspectives. I have received as much as I have given. I have learnt from others and from my own mistakes the best way to handle other people's anger. By exploring the psychology behind

INTRODUCTION

our emotions, I have identified different triggers and certain techniques that will help us to manage these triggers.

It is now time to share all that I have learnt and allow others to experience the same relief that I have. Having first-hand experience of that feeling like the world is out to get you, I now know that it isn't, and I want to help you reach the same understanding.

Together, we are going to explore all of the aspects of anger. We will look at the source, from our childhoods to the current situations that have caused the need to seek anger management. We will also take a closer look at domestic violence. It's a terribly isolating experience that is often hard to accept but know that you are not alone and that you can survive and thrive, and we are going to look at exactly how to do this and the help that is available for you.

It might be that your anger has come about because of some type of trauma or grief. It could be your children who have anger issues, and you fear that they are heading down a dangerous path. There is nothing wrong with needing some help every now and then, especially when it comes to something as critical as our emotions and the emotions of those who play a major part in our lives.

It's not hard to find a book on anger management. What is hard is to find one that has been written for women, by a

INTRODUCTION

woman who has lived through the trauma caused by anger. It's true that while we all have different reactions, secondary emotions, and triggers, there is still a significant difference between men and women when it comes to anger. This isn't me being a feminist or sexist, science tells us that men and women experience anger differently. While many of the causes and triggers can be related to both sexes, our attention is going to be on women and how we can learn to understand our strong emotions and manage them.

My hope with this book is that together we can gain a better understanding of anger, the root causes, and the triggers. We will explore the brain and find out just what goes on when rage starts to build up inside us. It is also important to look into the impact of grief and trauma in our lives and how it relates to anger.

There are so many dynamics in our friendships and relationships. It is certainly not uncommon for us to have to deal with an angry teenager. Others have to suffer with angry partners which can manifest into verbal or physical abuse. If you feel like you are living in an impossible situation, I understand, but we will look at ways to overcome this, seeking professional help if necessary.

Anger is a scary emotion, your own and other people's. That being said, there are ways that we can recognize this powerful emotion and learn to control it. Before we begin to

INTRODUCTION

learn how to manage our anger, let's discover exactly what it is.

1

WHAT IS ANGER?

From a very young age, we learn what anger is. It's the emotion that can make us shout or cry. It's what makes your toddler throw themselves on the floor and scream just because you said no to Peppa Pig for the 20th time. But ask yourself if you can define it. It's one of those words that is much easier to spot than it is to describe.

Anger is a strong emotion that is caused by a negative situation or by a feeling that someone has done you wrong. It may arise from others provoking you, hurting you, or feeling as if you are threatened or are in danger. There are varying degrees of anger. It could be relatively mild, that irritable feeling when our basic human needs aren't met- when we are hungry or tired. We often become angry when someone criticizes us. When someone deliberately goes out of their way to hurt us, we may become furious.

YASMIN A.

Anger can also stem from other emotions and in this case, it is known as a secondary emotion. Have you ever noticed how you scare someone, and they respond in anger. Or might feel sad or lonely which develops into frustration and anger.

While these are the non-physical symptoms of anger, there are a number of physical reactions that help us to identify anger. In others, we witness shouting, swearing, or high levels of sarcasm. In ourselves, muscles begin to tense across our body, our heart rate increases, and some people struggle with headaches.

You may have seen just how destructive anger can be. Families are torn apart, the once loving happy atmosphere is replaced with tension and bitterness. Taking anger out on children is soul-destroying and bit by bit, you notice them walking with their heads that little bit lower, no longer laughing spiritedly. Eventually, anger issues result in pushing everyone away from us, so we are alone.

On a more wide-scale note, anger prevents learning. When we are unable to learn about other people's cultures, perspectives, values, and beliefs, we see crowds of people turn into mobs, mobs become conflict and conflicts become a war.

What Are the Causes of Anger?

The human brain fascinates me. We often take its power and complexities for granted. I have had many days where I feel like my brain is not working, but not only does it never stop, it rarely gets a chance to rest.

An extensive study was carried out in Valencia with regards to what happens to the brain when we get angry. On the one hand, our heart rate, arterial tension, and testosterone levels increase. On the other hand, the stress hormone, cortisol, decreases. The effect of anger on the brain is a change in the asymmetries of the brain.

The results of the study showed that anger doesn't resemble other emotions. The left frontal area of the brain is associated with our positive emotions and the negative emotions to the right. But we also categorize our emotions as those that provoke closeness and those that provoke withdrawal. Our close emotions are those like happiness and logically, withdrawal comes about from fear and other negative emotions. It is the left frontal area that handles our closeness emotions and the right for withdrawal. Up to now, this makes sense, left side positive and close, right side negative and withdrawal. Anger is a negative emotion, but it is also associated with closeness, we often want to get close to the source of our anger so we can get rid of it.

YASMIN A.

Anger also impacts our cardiovascular system in more ways than increasing our heart rate. Our blood pressure increases, as does our blood glucose levels and blood fatty acid level. Over time, this can lead to clogged and damaged blood vessels and even heart attacks. Our immune system has a lower number of natural killer cells and a higher number of virus-infected cells. Our metabolism is lower, and anger can even increase intraocular pressure, affecting our eyesight.

Science can help us with part of the understanding but there still has to be a cause for this chemical and physical reaction. As mentioned before, it might be that someone has hurt you or you are feeling the pressure of a long day and it's more difficult to control your temper. Some people express frustration or aggression when they are unable to express themselves clearly.

Social situations are a frequent source, especially when you look at schools where children are still learning those essential communication skills. Both the bully and the victim can have anger management issues. An angry child in one surrounding could be the sign of an abused child in a different setting. Stress, anxiety, depression, and PTSD are all psychological causes of anger. Anger can become incredibly difficult to manage when a person has a history of trauma, more specifically, sexual abuse. Medical conditions such as drug or alcohol addiction, mental disabilities, and biochemical changes can all cause anger.

Let's take a look at some specific examples:

- **Frustration-** a teenager can't do their homework and shouts at their parents or an adult who is trying to assemble a new table and throws the instructions across the room.
- **A lack of power-** when people are all talking over you and making decisions without consulting you and you raise your voice and slam your hands on the table.
- **Threatened-** in situations when we feel threatened, the fight or flight response kicks in and we often become angry as a way of fighting the threat.
- **Lack of respect-** those who are in a position of authority may lose their patience and show signs of anger when this authority is not respected, for example, teachers or police.
- **Not respecting boundaries-** siblings will often start to shout and fight when one is not playing according to the expectations and boundaries of the other.
- **Impolite behavior-** rude drivers, arrogant shop

assistants, your kids not saying please and thank you- or my favorite, when you hold the door open for a stranger and they don't say thank you.
- **Demanding people-** your boss or colleague is expecting too much from you and you lash out.
- **Lack of appreciation-** it's common to become angry with your family when you have worked all day, cleaned up after everyone, cooked, cleaned again and there is little thanks.
- **As a response to anger-** a conversation becomes heated, the other person shows signs of anger and because a lot of our communication mirrors what the other person is doing, we become angry.
- **Envy and jealousy-** the co-worker who gets the promotion that you wanted or your parents unfairly comparing you to your siblings.
- **Helplessness-** when you feel out of depth at work or your friend is in a hopeless situation, this frustration can soon become anger.

Anger in the workplace is particularly challenging as we spend so much time there. Generally speaking, we are better at managing our emotions at work and the problems we have at home tend to stay there. However, it is not so easy to compartmentalize the negative emotions we experience at work and they often seep into our personal and family life. This is even more noticeable with modern technology. Emails and messages come through 24 hours a day and it's hard not to get angry with such pressure.

You can probably list a hundred more scenarios, but you get my drift. We are living in very tense times with too much stress and pressure on ourselves, and not just adults. While children and young adults can get angry for unnecessary reasons, there are still plenty of justifiable causes for their anger.

THE 10 DIFFERENT TYPES OF ANGER

It was Shakespeare who said, "There is nothing either good or bad but thinking makes it so". Anger is very much like this. We are quick to assume that it is bad, but this isn't necessarily the case. In some cases, anger can be good. The right amount of anger can motivate us to achieve what we want. Anger is simply just anger, even our brains can't limit it to a positive or negative emotion. Anger is only bad or good when we label it in that way.

Some experts categorize anger in three main groups, others have more. Here is a thorough list of different types of anger that we can experience:

1. **Assertive Anger** - You can view this as a constructive type of anger, and it prevents us from bottling up our feelings that can cause the situation to become worse later on. Assertive anger allows you to express your wants and needs without crossing the boundaries of others.
2. **Behavioral Anger** - This anger is intentional, extreme, and often hurts another person. This could be by throwing or breaking things and causing fear or physically hurting the other person. It is highly aggressive anger.
3. **Chronic Anger** - When the anger starts to become more persistent, it is known as chronic anger. It's that feeling you get when absolutely everything irritates you and you are frustrated by most things in life. And the name suggests, the length of time associated with chronic anger can lead to serious health issues.
4. **Judgmental Anger** - If you feel a sense of injustice or that somebody else's flaws are not acceptable, you become judgmental. You may feel that you are better than other people or in certain cases, that you are not as good as others.
5. **Overwhelmed Anger** - This often comes from feeling out of control. It might be because of the huge amount of responsibilities we have or that we

have taken on more than we can handle. When life throws us too many challenges, the stress becomes too much, and we become angry.

6. **Passive-aggressive anger** - Your anger could be expressed by giving people the silent treatment, you may be sarcastic to the point of mocking people. Passive-aggressive people will often play the victim. It is a tactic to avoid coping with feelings and can have severe consequences on our relationships.

7. **Retaliation Anger** - If someone comes across as angry or aggressive, you will respond with anger. This is one of the most common types of anger and though not always it can sometimes be deliberate. However, it may also be impulsive.

8. **Verbal Anger** - Shouting, screaming, insulting, swearing, harsh criticism are just some examples of verbal anger. It can appear to be less dangerous, but it will still cause immense pain to the person who is receiving the verbal abuse.

9. **Volatile Anger** - This is another form of impulsive anger and it may even catch you unaware. It seems to quickly appear from nowhere. People will tread very carefully around you and will find it difficult to express how they feel as they will fear your possible outbursts.

10. **Self-Abusive Anger** - The anger that you feel towards yourself can be in the form of negative self-talk and/or self-harm. In certain cases, it is associated with substance abuse or eating disorders. Your extremely low self-esteem can cause you to push others further away by being angry at them.

WHAT TRIGGERS ANGER?

Well, it's a good question that can have any number of answers. My husband got angry the other day because of a fly. My teenager got angry because I made her wash up. My colleague got angry because a meeting ran late. Triggers are unique to each person. If a fly lands in my food I don't shout, but my husband's intolerance for this annoying little insect is as if he has been told his car had been stolen.

Some typical triggers that are enough to trigger most of us include:

- Disrespect of space
- Disrespect of values or opinions
- Lies
- Being interrupted
- Accusations
- Insults and/or threats
- Other people's ignorance or even stupidity

- Impatience

Though there are plenty more, it is up to you to uncover your triggers. You might be able to quickly rattle off a list of things that make you angry, however, there are probably other things that you aren't aware of until they come up.

My advice at this stage would be to use an anger track sheet that you can keep with you for a week or a month and track the different types of anger and your triggers. It would be helpful if you could keep a note of the time of day as well, as this will help you to recognize any patterns.

The alternative is to keep a journal. Writing your feelings in a journal is one of the best ways to become more aware of not only anger but all of your emotions. At the end of the day, you can take a few minutes to make a note of the triggers that made you angry. Over a short period of time, much like with the worksheet, you will be able to get a clearer understanding of what your triggers are. Remember that triggers are something that regularly causes you to become angry. Look for secondary emotions before you assume it is a trigger. You might find that the shopping bag breaking isn't a trigger, you were just angry because you were already having a bad day, the bag was the icing on the cake.

Due to the intricate nature of anger and the variety of personalities, the answer to the question "What is Anger?"

could almost be a book on its own. The types and triggers are so personal that it is almost insulting to put a label on anger other than 'a strong emotional feeling'.

Even cultural differences play their role. During my holidays in Spain, I would watch with a jaw-dropping expression as people on the streets were aggressively waving their hands around while talking to others. I thought it must have been some serious disagreement. But when it happened over and over again, I soon learnt that rather than being a confrontational nation, they are just very expressive with their hands. A warm hug is acceptable in some countries but can enrage those in others.

It's hard to imagine a human being on earth who hasn't experienced some form of anger. In many cases, we accept it as a normal part of life. Nevertheless, in cases like ours, anger management is essential if we are going to learn how to live happier, more fulfilling lives. There will also be a need to understand if and when professional help is required. And this is what we are going to explore in the next chapter.

2

HOW CAN I BECOME BETTER AT MANAGING MY ANGER?

One of the hardest things I have had to learn is anger management. Count to 10 is probably the most common advice we have received and there is a good reason for this, but it's just a drop in the anger management ocean. It's one thing to recognize your angry emotions and know what you should do. It's a completely different thing to master the control.

For decades, the world has paid so much attention to intelligence. From the youngest of ages, children are tested on their ability to store information and judged by this. No child is tested on their ability to express their feelings or share with friends, both essential skills that need to be learnt.

In 1990, Peter Salovey and John Mayer coined the term Emotional Intelligence, which later became known as EQ or Emotional Quotient. This is the ability to monitor your feelings and the feelings of others and use the information to help develop your thoughts and actions. Throughout the 90s, we also saw social behaviors being incorporated into EQ, for example, the ability to manage your own emotions, to be understanding towards other people's feelings, and to deal with their emotions.

Like intelligence, not everyone is a master at Emotional Intelligence, and it is something that we need to learn and practice. However, emotionally intelligent people know how to manage their anger.

5 THINGS AN EMOTIONALLY INTELLIGENT PERSON DOES WHEN THEY ARE ANGRY

In the first place, emotionally intelligent people know that it is bad to react to anger. Whether it's your own or somebody else's, quick responses rarely resolve anything. Instead, it fuels the situation and appears defensive. To prevent themselves from responding and coming across as defensive, they will follow these 5 steps:

1. **Stop!** - It goes back to counting to 10. There is a very good reason why this cliché has survived the

test of time. When anger begins to boil up inside us, the first thing to do is stop, take a very deep breath, and count to 10. This prevents us from responding too fast. When we allow anger to hijack our rational and logical brain, we don't have time to appreciate what triggered the emotion in the first place.

2. **Ask "Why"** - Why are you angry? If someone steals your parking spot are you angry because now you are going to be late, or because you are going to have to walk further in the rain? When you constantly have to pick up after your partner and your kids, does the anger come from having to repeat yourself or from the fact that you feel completely abused in your role as wife/girlfriend/mom? Look for secondary emotions that come with your anger.

3. **What else is going on when you feel angry?** - I feel terrible when I snap at my family because of the pressure of work. It's not their fault but there are so many things going on in our heads that it is hard to keep everything under control. Check that your basic needs are met. Are you hungry, angry about something else, lonely, or tired. Have you been disappointed and it's coming out as anger?

4. **Show Empathy** - The ability to show empathy

means you can understand why the other person has become angry. If you haven't taken a step back to breathe and understand why you are angry, it will be even harder to see things from the other person's point of view. We aren't alone in our suffering. Our colleagues may also be having a nightmare at home or our mum has a ton of other problems which cause them to have secondary emotions such as anger. Showing empathy is not the same as excusing them for their outburst. It will help you to be more aware of how the other person feels.

5. **Use "I" statements** - This is a favorite technique for those who want to assert themselves. When you use sentences like "I feel hurt when you shout at me" rather than "You hurt me when you shout at me", it keeps the focus on expressing your emotions. Beginning a sentence with you can lead the other person to feel as if you are blaming them for your emotions.

When first learning to manage my anger, it would amuse me when professionals explained these 5 steps. I mean, how are you supposed to process all of this in between the trigger and the response? Luckily, our brain acts faster than reading so in the time it takes to count to 10, it has the ability to consider all.

Still, reading how emotionally intelligent people handle anger and learning how to do this does take a little time. It is also great for those moments of rage but what about when your whole life just feels angry. Let's look at how we can relieve the sense of fury from our day to day lives.

Learn How to Say No

It can get pretty frustrating when people are always asking you to do things and you reluctantly say yes. Even if they are small jobs, they start to eat away at the time you would prefer to be doing other things. Many of us fear saying no because we don't want to upset the other person, or we feel guilty for putting ourselves first. But the end result is we are constantly angry.

Learning how to say no doesn't make us selfish or unkind. We can say no in an assertive way that is still friendly and perfectly reasonable. Practice some simple sentences like "I can't today, sorry" or "I'm afraid that's not going to work for me". Don't feel obliged to offer explanations and remember that it is your right to say no to things you don't want to do. If people put pressure on you, tell them you will think about it and take some time to decide if their request is one that won't add to your already heavy load.

YASMIN A.

Focus on Making Yourself Happy

Excuse me? My happiness? Take time for me? Women are shocked by the thought. But how frustrating is it that your husband comes home from work and puts his feet up while you keep going. Not all men are like this, but it happens more than we would like to think. This can infuriate any normal person.

I'm not suggesting whole days out on your own or popping off to the movies while your family is left to fend for themselves. It is more than reasonable for you to take 20 minutes to exercise or take a shower without interruptions. When talking to a child once, I asked what their mom's hobbies were. The child said, "My mom's hobby is cleaning". Women can have hobbies that go beyond the cooking and the ironing! Find your passions. Start by taking 5 minutes then 10 and gradually build up to an appropriate amount of time for you to be happy.

Keep a Journal

Writing down things that you might be afraid to tell others or that you don't want others to know is a great way to process how you feel. You can keep track of secondary emotions and pay attention to what triggers your anger. It's a good way to practice expressing how you feel before you talk to others. If you don't feel like you can talk to anyone, keeping a journal might be essential.

Exercise and Sleep

I love exercise because even after 10 or 15 minutes doing Zumba on my Wii I feel like a happier, healthier person and this gives me the extra confidence I need to face my challenges. Whether it's an hour at the gym, a walk in the park, or yoga, exercise releases endorphins that naturally help us to calm down. Exercise helps you to sleep better, so you will feel more refreshed in the mornings. I know that waking up tired doesn't put me in the best of moods.

Let Yourself Break Once in a While

It is ok to cry. Crying doesn't make us weak, nor should you feel overly sensitive or dramatic. On the contrary, it can help you to let go of some of that anger that has been building up inside you. Cry on a friend's shoulder or your partner's. Put those meaningful songs on and cry alone. Studies have shown that crying can not only help to self-sooth, but it can also release oxytocin and endorphins, the chemicals that make us feel good.

THE USE OF RELAXATION TECHNIQUES FOR ANGER MANAGEMENT

In no way is this a sob-story but some years ago I couldn't relax. It wasn't a case of getting a little bit fidgety or that I raced around doing everything at full speed. I just couldn't stop. My day would begin at around 7 am if I was lucky and I would finish work at 11 pm. If it wasn't work, it would be folding clothes, tidying up or getting ready for the next day.

It hit me when I went out with some friends for coffee and the stress of not doing anything was too much for me. I was literally peering into their cups to see if they had finished. My leg was twitching, and it wasn't impossible to focus on the conversation, only the list of things I should have been doing. It was then that I knew I had to teach myself how to relax.

My research was fruitful. I was assuming that I was going to have to learn how to do nothing, but I was pleased to find activities that would engage my brain so that I didn't feel guilty for doing "nothing". Here are some of the relaxation techniques I found to be extremely beneficial.

Yoga- There are so many different types of yoga and even more ways to practice it. Zen Yoga combines yoga, Zen, breathing techniques and flexibility. Yoga Nidra is a form of guided meditation where you can enjoy a state of sleep while awake. Yoga is great because you can do it anywhere, anytime. Or you can join a group which will help you break your useful routine, even feel like an adult for a while.

Deep Breathing- This involves long, deep breaths but without your chest rising. Instead, we contract the diaphragm, allowing our belly to expand and then contract. You can inhale for a count to ten, and exhale for the same amount of time for 10 to 15 times each day.

Meditation- Like yoga, there are many types of meditation. You practice by focusing on one object or one thought. The focus must be complete with all of your attention. Meditation can help reduce stress levels. Studies show that 8 minutes a day can bring about positive benefits, however there are some, like Transcendental Meditation requires 20 minutes, twice a day, depending on the chants you use with it.

Tai Chi- Tai Chi is a series of slow controlled movements along with deep breathing. Your body is constantly moving, and it really does work the muscles.

YASMIN A.

Progressive muscle relaxation- By gradually working through each muscle in the body, tightening and relaxing each one, you learn to appreciate the difference between tension and relaxation. I found it helped to identify muscles that I didn't even realize were tense because I was so used to it.

Visualization- In order for visualization to work, you need to truly believe in the image you create. Imagine yourself in calming surroundings, feeling happy and relaxed. Soak up the sounds and smells of the environment. This brings peace to your mind as you replace negative thoughts with positive images.

Biofeedback- For those who love modern technology, Biofeedback is the ability to learn more about what is happening with the help of electronics.

Music and Art Therapy- Music and Art Therapy is a type of therapy that encourages self-expression and self-soothing. You don't have to be good at it, I'm certainly not, but it does help to let go of some of those feelings we keep inside of us.

Aromatherapy- Scientists believe that breathing in the scent of essential oils activates your smell receptors and sends messages through your nerves to your brain. Find an essential oil that makes you feel positive and try to make sure that it is 100% plant extract.

Don't be afraid to explore your own relaxation techniques. You may not believe this but ironing actually relaxes me, not when I have to do it, but putting on my favorite series and doing something that doesn't require any concentration is a nice job for me. Not everything works for the same people. Some people find certain techniques more stressful than relaxing. There is no right or wrong here.

PROFESSIONAL HELP FOR ANGER MANAGEMENT

At times, our anger becomes too much for us to handle and this is ok too. If you have tried some techniques to handle your anger and nothing seems to be helping, it doesn't mean you have failed or that there is no hope. As we have said, the brain is a mighty complex organ and sometimes it needs help to process all of our thoughts, actions, feelings, and experiences.

There is not a lot of different types of help available and it's not just about laying on the couch and talking about your feelings. Professional help could be with a type of exercise that helps you master one of the relaxation techniques. Perhaps you want to use art as an outlet for your anger and you would like some classes. Then, of course there are types of therapies that will help you with anger management.

Two common types of therapy used by professionals are rational emotive behavioral therapy and cognitive behavioral therapy.

RATIONAL EMOTIVE BEHAVIORAL THERAPY (REBT)

Professionals will use REBT as a way to help you recognize thoughts and feelings that are self-defeating. Self-defeating thoughts are those that make you feel as if you are doomed to fail. They can also lead to negative behaviors such as drinking, smoking, and not leading a healthy life. REBT allows you to challenge the negative thoughts with rational logic. Not only is it used to help with anger and aggression, but it can also help reduce stress, anxiety, and depression. We will look closer at REBT a little later on.

COGNITIVE BEHAVIORAL THERAPY (CBT)

CBT is a type of talking therapy but rather than focusing on problems from the past, it looks at the problems you are suffering from in the present. It enables you to work through your thoughts and feelings by breaking down the larger problems into smaller, more manageable ones. CBT helps you to decide if your thoughts and feelings are unrealistic or unhelpful and how they can have a negative effect on your life.

HOW DO I KNOW IF I NEED PROFESSIONAL HELP?

I know I needed help when I began to see the effect my anger was having on my family. You may notice the same, or perhaps it is negatively impacting your friendships or your career. If you feel like you are in an impossible situation and there is no way out, it is definitely time to ask for help. Here are some other signs of that it could be time to get help:

- You are passive-aggressive- though not as obvious as bursts of anger, it is still something that causes a lot of pain.
- You constantly blame others- this means you are struggling to take responsibility for your own actions.
- You are aggressive- whether it's physical or verbal, your loved ones as well as yourself are going to suffer.
- Your anger is not in proportion to the problem- when your child accidentally drops their dinner, and you fly off the handle is just one example.

- Your anger is too often and lasts for too long - anger from time to time is normal but when it begins to take over life, it's a bigger problem.

On the other hand, you might be on the receiving end of someone else's anger. If you fear someone you love because of their temper, physical or verbal, you need to get help, even if it is just taking the first step and talking to someone.

You will be able to find a printable self-rating tick sheet to get a better understanding of whether you should seek professional help. You can click on the links below for recognized organizations that can help you.

> National Anger Management Association (USA)
> https://namass.org/index.html
>
> National Alliance on Mental Illness (USA)
> https://www.nami.org/Home
>
> Lifeline (Australia)
> https://www.lifeline.org.au
>
> Bell Let's Talk (Canada)
> https://letstalk.bell.ca/en/get-help/

NHS (UK)
https://www.nhs.uk/conditions/stress-anxiety-depression/mental-health-helplines/

It's important to remember that you are not alone. It's also essential that you don't get sucked into the stigma and connotations associated with mental illnesses. Anger is a symptom of mental illness like depression and addictive behaviors. You are not crazy! Quite the opposite, seeking help from a mental illness professional is the smart step to take. A lot of these websites have contact numbers where you can talk to professionals and even apps, text chat and video chat. Talking to an outsider who is not there to judge but listen to you, can often be a huge step forward in managing your anger.

3

ANGER AND THE GENDER DIFFERENCES

Before we get right into these gender differences; I strongly want to reiterate that we are talking about men and women in general. There are men who are calmer than women, more affectionate, and even better at expressing their emotions. There are also men who are better househusbands and better parents. At the same time, there are women who are better at business. I know women who can make furniture, fix their own car, put up new shelves. Nobody can be simply put into a box and labelled. I don't like it when people do that to me so I'm not about to do it to the rest of the world.

We are born equal. Maybe that is what is so amazing about newborns. You hold this little person knowing that there is a clean canvass in front of you. They are yet to be influenced by society and its beliefs. They haven't watched the Disney films where the princess needs to be rescued by the prince or watched the TV and movies that depict how life should be. Then you have the toddler stage when they start to express their emotions. All they do is tell it how it is, they don't care if they are a little boy or a little girl. They shout, cry, and stomp their feet. It's a difficult time for parents and naturally something that children have to learn, but to some extent, I am envious of these little people who can truly express how they feel.

As we continue to grow up, the influences start to have an impact on who we are. It's an unspoken rule in society; women aren't allowed to be angry. Sometimes I wonder if it goes back to before the feminist revolution of the 60s. Our role as a housewife was to take care of the children, cook and clean. We didn't have to go to the office or worry about money. Our lives were seen, as far easier, much less stressful and there was no need for us to get angry. We didn't have goals so there was no frustration when they weren't achieved. Those that did want to do more with their lives were almost ridiculed. It hurts even to type the words, but I wonder how many of our moms and grandmothers had to hear the words "But you're just a woman"!

Luckily, so much has changed yet we still aren't "allowed" to express our anger. Looking back over some of the most popular movies in the last couple of decades, can you think of one where a woman shows her anger for good reason, but the scene is portrayed in the right context? They are crazy, jealous, out for revenge, ill, confused, but never just angry. Take Julia Roberts in the all-time, classic Pretty Woman, she had every right to be angry after the way she was treated by one man, instead, she cried and struggled to get her words out. There are numerous examples of this still today.

Still, these are just my humble observations. So, let's see what science tells us. We have to bear in mind that there are so many studies on anger differences between the genders. I will cover as many as possible so that we reduce the chance of bias.

NATURE VS NURTURE

The social-developmental hypothesis is the correct term for my blank canvass newborn idea. It argues that a newborn isn't aware of gender differences and emotional expression. Our children learn by watching parents and other adults around them. Generally speaking, once they reach toddler age, parents talk to girls about emotions more than they do boys. This leaves an imprint on the child that they take with them into teenage years, and it affects how they treat their friends. As you might expect, it can also carry through into our relationships.

Society's influences continue to play a role in the social-developmental hypothesis. We act how we feel we should act to fit in with what is expected. Women are encouraged to express and show feelings such as love, care, and comfort. Men on the other hand are discouraged from expressing such emotions. When it comes to anger, it is vice versa, men should show it, women shouldn't. Young children watching adult behavior will grow up to fit into these gender roles.

Take for example, a group of children playing. It is still typical to see girls to be sat down calmly, at a nice make-believe tea party or playing with dolls. Their play is emotional and caring. Boys, however, may be more likely to be physically active, running around, jumping, shouting, there is an element of competition in their play, even aggression. A lot of effort is being made to change this, particularly in the classrooms, but when Christmas comes again, pay attention to all of the adverts with girls playing with pink "homely" toys and the boys with their blue transformers. It still happens. Our children are socialized into emotional or unemotional gender roles.

While this theory helps us to understand the expression of emotions, it doesn't explain what actually happens in the brain of men and women when anger strikes.

YASMIN A.

DO MEN AND WOMEN EXPERIENCE EMOTIONS DIFFERENTLY?

The problem with the question is that in order to carry out studies, scientists and researchers have to heavily rely on self-reports. So, the data collected tells us how that person felt in a certain situation. It's extremely hard to make solid conclusions when each person, and the brain, is so different. If we all watched a horror movie, the emotions that we report aren't going to be conclusive because you might find the movie a little jumpy and I might be hiding behind the sofa.

One study was carried out where males and females watched a video of other people being hurt. When looking at the information from the self-reports, the women showed far more empathy than men did. However, when the researchers compared physiological responses, there was no difference in blood pressure, heart rate, or pupil dilation. This study implied that our bodies do the same things but how we report it is different.

A different study involved men and women seeing a range of images and each person noting how the image made them feel. At the same time, MRI brain scans were carried out. The scans showed a difference in the neural circuitry during different emotional reactions.

For women, the activity is presented in the insula cortex (a lobe located in both hemispheres of the brain and processes bodily sensations). This means that the emotions women feel are deeply rooted in their bodies. For men, the neural activity presented in the visual cortex (the part of the brain that processes visual information received). In summary, women take their emotions deep inside them whereas men are more capable of reflecting their emotions back away from them.

The examples of these two studies show that the answer is far from simple and a question that will continue to spark controversy and new research. One final thought that makes logical sense goes back to the very early days of humans and our natural instincts as cavemen and cavewomen.

PREHISTORIC MAN, BIOLOGICAL MAKEUP AND HORMONES

Going back to the natural fight or flight instinct can provide us with another interpretation to how men and women differ with their emotions. The amygdala is a group of cells close to the base of our brains. There is one connected to the left hemisphere and another connected to the right. It's the amygdala that kicks out the instinct to run when we face a fear or stay and fight it out.

YASMIN A.

Because of the extra estrogen in a woman's brain, our brains tell us that it is safer to stay in groups, which we saw back in the times of prehistoric man. Within the group, women don't only feel safer, but stress is reduced and with lower amounts of testosterone, we are better at finding solutions to conflicts. Together, women would protect themselves and the children from danger. It also offers an explanation as to why we are more able to pick up on other people's emotions as we are more inclined to spend time together.

The testosterone in a man's brain drives him to compete. He must compete for food and more importantly, for a mate, if he wishes to pass on his genes. Men were isolated from the group while off hunting, they learnt how to adapt to social distancing from the groups. On top of this, the male amygdala has testosterone receptors which can increase the emotional responses to danger.

Again, it is very general, but this would explain why when a woman is upset, she seeks comfort in other women, or even groups. But, when men are upset, they tend to retreat to be alone.

To add to this, studies also show that men and women display their emotions for different lengths of time and at different frequencies. Again, after studying the different facial expressions of men and women while watching a range of TV ads, scientists were able to conclude that women smile more frequently than men and for longer. But this wasn't all, the number of times women raised their inner eyebrows (a sign of fear and sadness) was more often than men. However, eyebrow furrowing (which points to anger) was more frequent in men and lasted for longer.

HOW DO THESE DIFFERENCES AFFECT OUR FAMILY LIVES?

Our emotions play a large part in our communication, there is no doubting that. When we are angry, we can consciously try to communicate in a positive way, but our subconscious has the ability to portray our true feelings. This might be with subtle movements with our body language or micro facial expressions.

What started off as an observation could be met with criticism, in response to the criticism, a partner may express contempt or sarcasm, and before we are aware, an innocent comment has turned into a full-blown argument. Defensiveness, sarcasm, hostility, and withdrawal are the four characteristics of marital distress, collectively known as the 'four horsemen'. It is contempt that relates to our topic as contempt is described as a combination of disgust and anger. When anger progresses to contempt, the toxicity of a relationship is too much for either to bear and will often lead to the end of the relationship.

YASMIN A.

While we aren't going to place blame on anyone nor try to make anyone feel guilty, contempt has also been linked to childhood traumatic experiences. When children grow up in a toxic environment, witnessing contempt between their parents, and even parents who view their children with contempt, can grow up to experience problematic relationships themselves.

As difficult as it is, there will come a point in your learning about anger and anger management when you have to decide whether your problems with anger are the cause of the problems in your relationship or whether the situation has gone beyond this and it's time to part ways.

Though it is you who is suffering, there are two people in every relationship and so if yours is coming to an end, it's not just your fault. If you have tried talking to your husband or partner about your problems and they have not responded or are not making an effort to help you, then it might be time to consider the next stages of your journey without them. You are stronger than you think, and you will be able to do it.

Having said that, if you haven't spoken to your partner, it is definitely time, so that you can work on finding a solution together. Your partner may have taken your outbursts personally instead of understanding that you have a problem. Nothing is over until you have calmly talked to each other, using "I" statements, cry, and let it all out.

"Yesterday I cried. Must have been relief to see the softer side"

— **MEREDITH BROOKS**

WHAT TO MAKE OF ALL OF THESE STUDIES

It's hard to provide any simple answer when it comes to the emotions felt and experienced by men and women. There are too many external influences behind it. For example, what if participants in the studies had secondary emotions. What if some smiled more because the image reminded them of their child? Or they were angry because the same thing had once happened to them.

There is enough evidence to support the idea that men and women express their emotions differently. Whether that is because of our biological makeup or society's influence, or both, we don't express our anger in the same way.

The studies may not interest everyone and that's fine. I always like to mention it because it helps me to put things in context. When my husband used to have sudden outbursts of rage, I would imagine him as a caveman wandering alone in the wild, hunting for our food. This gave me an almost humorous mental image that helped me not to retaliate. It also allowed me to show empathy, it must be hard for men to feel like they can't express their sadness, as much as it is hard for us not to be able to express our anger.

While we can now understand why there is a difference between the genders, it doesn't mean that there is a decent excuse. Not all anger is bad and, in some cases, it can be healthier to express your anger, so it's not fair that women still aren't able to do so without being labeled.

4

IS THERE SUCH A THING AS HEALTHY ANGER?

It sounds like an oxymoron, the words healthy and anger don't seem to fit together, as if they are two opposite ends of a magnet. The truth is, not all anger is bad. In fact, anger is neither good nor bad until you make it one of the two.

We have to accept that in life, we are going to get angry. None of us are saints and life is going to continue throwing challenges at us that will stir up negative emotions, even when we have learnt to handle them correctly.

We have looked at what is considered to be unhealthy anger. Moments when you lash out either physically or verbally are never going to be considered healthy anger. Neither is passive aggression, raising your voice or throwing things in rage. However, healthy anger is the ability to recognize it as a tool to better understand why you are responding to something in such a way.

When you consider that you aren't going to be able to get rid of it but at the same time, it's unhealthy not being able to control it, our options start to become more limited. This is when, particularly as women, we tend to push this anger back down as a way of suppressing it. And no, this isn't healthy either. Repressing anger can have significant negative consequences on your health. Suppressed anger can lead to anxiety and depression, which will have a knock-on-effect on your relationships. It has also been linked to headaches, skin disorders, digestive problems, high blood pressure, and heart problems. Studies have also shown that hiding your anger increases your risk of bronchitis and heart attacks.

Getting the balance between healthy and unhealthy anger is essential for both our physical and mental health as well as our relationships.

As with many things in life, society goes from one extreme to the other before we are able to determine this balance. During the 60s, the world saw great rebellion against so many things, suppressing anger being one of them. Therapists throughout the 70s promoted the idea that the healthiest way to express our anger was to verbally let it all out or to get it all off your chest. One can see how this must have been quite refreshing for women who had been so used to hiding their emotions. Nevertheless, this was one of the negative extremes. Professionals later determined that the practice of letting your anger out only added fuel to the fire. It increased our own stress levels and made those around us respond in anger.

What happened during the 80s and 90s still puzzles me. Women went from expressing their anger in the 70s but slowly, we fell back into the unwritten rules of society and began to put a lid back on those intense feelings. Men on the other hand, continued to express their anger freely. Even today, we can still see this trend in social media, particularly with political posts and tweets. It's more common for male politicians to appear angry and aggressive, even resorting to insults and cyberbullying. Whereas again female politicians are still seen as more civil. This is painful for me to watch. As much as we are trying to bring about equality between the two genders, those who yield the most power in the world are setting negative examples for the youth of today, who spend so much time on social media.

HOW TO RECOGNIZE HEALTHY ANGER

Anger is healthy when you are able to recognize it for what it is, and it doesn't lead you to become overwhelmed. Instead of responding to anger in a negative way, we can take this anger and use it to examine our thoughts, feelings, and how our body reacts to it. Anger normally arises because one of our needs hasn't been met. Healthy anger means we are able to identify that need or desire.

There is a certain level of compassion required for healthy anger. Not just compassion towards yourself but also for those around you. By asserting yourself in the right way, you can communicate your feelings which makes it much easier to let go of them, forgiving ourselves and others.

Letting go of anger isn't the same as suppressing anger. Letting go means you have taken the time to process your feelings and you have gained awareness of the situation. Suppressing it is just pushing it back in its box.

Let's look at an example. Sandra has had a 10-hour shift at work and just at the end, her boss, shouts at her for something that wasn't her fault. She is angry but stores this in her metaphorical anger box. When she kids home, the kids haven't done their homework, they complain because mum is always a nag. Her frustration goes back in the box. Her husband is on the sofa, there are dirty dishes and no sign of dinner. She is now furious but still, the already full angry box is loaded with fury. One of two things are going to happen; the slightest thing is going to cause Sandra to explode or Sandra is going to go to bed. Exhaustion will take over and she will eventually fall asleep, only to start the same pattern again the next day.

Neither are the way any woman, or any human should have to live. If Sandra had processed her anger after her boss shouted, she would have been able to assert herself and explained the situation to her boss. This would have allowed her to return home happy and the buildup of each situation would have been easier to handle.

CAN EXPRESSING YOUR ANGER BE CONSTRUCTIVE

If we look at anger as across its varying degrees, we will go from suppression to violence or aggression. The healthy middle path is when we are able to recognize, understand, and process our anger, but there are still degrees of anger in between this and aggression. In fact, psychologists believe that only around 10% of the time we actually reach aggression. While it is better to have control over our anger, you shouldn't be too hard on yourself because expressing your anger can be constructive.

Studies have shown that between 40% and 55% of people agree that angry episodes have positive long-term effects. Angry outbursts can show someone how you are truly feeling and can often make the other person see things that they wouldn't have seen otherwise. In an ideal world, Sandra would have told her husband calmly but firmly that she doesn't appreciate coming home after a long day and have to

YASMIN A.

be responsible for everything in the house. We don't always live in this ideal world and perhaps Sandra did have an angry episode. Her husband may well have seen the seriousness of the situation and understood what he needs to do in the future.

Going back to my aunt who I talked about in the beginning of the book, she is the queen of healthy anger. She has mini explosions, everyone sits up and listens, she smiles and says, "I feel all better now". She also has many occasions where she manages her anger

and explains how she feels. But she doesn't punish herself for expressing her feelings when we all know she has reached her limit. In my humble opinion, this is a clear example of healthy anger in a real world where not every angry situation is going to be managed to perfection.

5

AN IN-DEPTH LOOK AT TRAUMA AND THE RELATIONSHIP WITH ANGER

In psychology, there are so many complex terms that help us to identify a certain emotion, disorder, or event, the spelling and pronunciation can often bewilder us. Then we come to the word trauma, and rarely understand the power and distress trauma causes. I tend to think that because it is such a simple term, we brush over the impacts of trauma and not realize the extent of the damage and the anger that trauma can cause us. Trauma can lead to many other psychological conditions, so it is important that we pay close attention to any form of trauma we suffer in our lives and learn how to deal with it.

Before looking at the causes of trauma, let's focus on the different types. Psychological trauma is when the mind has become damaged, often because of a distressing event or unbearable amounts of stress. Transgenerational trauma is one that is transferred down through the generations. Blunt trauma, or blunt force trauma, refers to physical injuries. Secondary trauma occurs when someone close to us has been traumatized and this has an impact on us. Major trauma can stem from one of the other forms of trauma and will cause long term disability or even death. Acts of crime can provoke one of the previously mentioned traumas or for example, we see perpetrator trauma, acts of terrible violence and rape trauma.

THE MAJOR CAUSES OF TRAUMA

Sexual Assault

Sexual assault refers to any form of sexual behavior that is not consensual. Rape is considered one of the worst types of trauma that a woman can experience because of the level of violation. That being said, any form of unwanted physical or verbal behavior in a sexual context is considered sexual assault. It is important to remember that this applies to relationships and marriages too.

Child Maltreatment

Child abuse can be physical or sexual. It can also be emotional or both physical and emotional neglect. Any form of physical pain or injury is physical abuse. Emotional abuse can range from verbal abuse, exceedingly high expectations, causing the child to create negative self-images, or emotional neglect, like not providing the necessary love and security. Sexual abuse isn't limited to intercourse, it can also be touching, kissing, genital exposure, verbal pressure for sex and sexual exploitation. Neglect is when the caregiver does not provide the required care from food to medical care. Neglect is also when caregivers expose children to dangerous environments or even not provide adequate supervision.

Domestic Violence

Domestic violence is any type of physical or emotional abuse between two people in a relationship. Insults, threatening physical abuse and sexual violence all fall under domestic violence. Though not as widely talked about it is possible for anger issues to cause women to carry out domestic violence.

War Related Trauma

Those who have suffered from living in a war zone experience massive trauma that is often linked to other causes. It can be bombing, shooting, or being forced to move from your home because of war. Terrorism causes trauma that more and more of us have suffered from in last two decades. From a different point of view, those soldiers who have had to engage in war and witness the tragedy can also suffer from post-traumatic stress disorder.

Racial Trauma

I still feel so much shock that this even exists in this day in age. Not only does it exist but acts of racism are getting more attention than ever and more violent acts, such as demonstrations, protests, and vandalism are arising because of it. There is still a huge amount of racism that goes undetected, in schools, the workplace, even in the media.

Natural Disasters

Tornadoes, earthquakes, hurricanes, and wildfires all have the potential to cause trauma from the loss of homes, even deaths of loved ones. In just a matter of minutes, people can have their entire lives turned upside down with nothing left except the clothes on their backs.

Divorce and Family Feuds

In severe cases, the struggles that we have in our relationships can cause trauma. Divorce, especially those that are 'messy' or where children are involved can bring about immense suffering for everyone involved. There have been family feuds which led to families not talking to each other for years, which is very traumatic.

Grief

Grief is also known as traumatic loss. It is when an adult or child loses someone close to them. More often than not, the death is rather sudden. Grief is probably the only type of trauma that we will all suffer from to a certain degree throughout our lives, so we will take a closer look at this now.

AN IN-DEPTH LOOK AT GRIEF

As I mentioned, losing 3 people who I was incredibly close to in such a short period of time makes me a bit of an expert with regards to the anger that grief can bring about. It was probably my sister passing away that I would associate with trauma. As if it's not bad enough losing my sister at what I would consider a young age, it was sudden and it also happened only one month after my sister in-law passed away. We were mourning her and supporting my brother and his children when my sister passed away too. It was tough as people were celebrating Christmas and New Year and our family was planning funerals.

Grief is the response we have when we lose someone that normally, we have been close to. Not all grief is the same. You might feel differently with the death of a parent to the death of a partner. The death of a pet is also a common cause of grieving. You might be surprised to learn that there are numerous types of grief, for example:

Anticipatory Grief- your loved one might have been suffering from a long-term illness and the death is anticipated. The grieving doesn't necessarily begin when the person dies, but when you accept that they are going to.

Complicated Grief- When grief is so overwhelming you struggle to lead a normal life. It may even lead to anxiety or depression.

Cumulative Grief- before processing the grief of one death, you lose someone else in your life, which is often called 'grief overload'.

Chronic Grief- stronger reactions to loss with little to no progress in working through the stages of grief.

Traumatic Grief- this is when a loved one has lost a person in a way that is frightening, unexpected, violent, or traumatic.

Absent Grief- you might associate this with denial. The person shows no sign of grief or they might be in shock for an extended period of time. It is quite common when the death of someone is sudden.

Collective Grief- a shared grief by a group of people or an entire nation. It is mostly associated with terrorist attacks, natural disasters, or maybe the death of a well-liked and respected public figure. The recent global health crisis is one example.

It's essential to remember that every person will experience grief differently. There are no long or hard rules on how to handle the death of a loved one. Don't think that you are doing it wrong or it shouldn't be taking so long. Just because you were anticipating it doesn't mean it is easier to overcome, and even if a whole group of people are grieving over the same loss, individuals will feel different types of emotions and at different levels. From first-hand experience, I can tell you that grief is not limited to one kind. My three losses provoked a long dark tunnel of grief, pain, and anger. In the space of just a few months, I experienced 5 of the six types of grief mentioned above.

WHAT DOES GRIEF LOOK LIKE?

Many people ask why they need to grieve or how long the process should take. As I said, there is no "should" when it comes to grieving, it will take as long as it takes. Rushing the process will likely cause you to not work through it correctly, prolonging the pain. On the other hand, assuming that "it will just pass" could mean that you don't fully process the loss.

I remember a friend who lost her grandmother who she was very close to. After a couple of weeks, she appeared absolutely fine. On the anniversary of her grandmother's death, she fell to pieces as if it had happened the day before. Nobody was expecting this, least of all my friend. It just goes to show that even if you think you are doing ok, you might not have worked through the grief completely.

After my second loss, I felt so angry and questioned why I needed to grieve, especially if this was going to keep happening. Somebody explained it to me in the most beautiful way and it still brings a tear to my eye.

With every relationship we create an energy that ties the two of us together. When someone passes away, you keep hold of this energy, even cling to it afraid that letting go means you will forget them. Really, we need to release this energy for two reasons. First, you need to focus on the energy in the ties that you have with those still living. Secondly, whether you choose to believe it or not, the loved one who passed away may need to take that energy with them. Grieving is the process of letting go of that energy so that we are not tied to the past and we can start replacing the pain with fond memories of the person you will always love.

THE FIVE STAGES OF GRIEF

When Kubler-Ross proposed the 5 stages of grief, it was not supposed to be interpreted as a way for people to deal with the loss of a person. It was a concept used to help terminally ill patients come to terms with what they were experiencing. Even she said that grief is unpredictable, and we can't all assume the same process will work for everyone.

Because we each experience grief differently, it's necessary to remember that the five stages of grief don't follow a tidy little pattern where we spend a week on each one before moving on to the next. The order of each stage can vary and so can the period of time for each. It is also true that some people can spend months in one stage but skip past the others. It's personal, so don't feel like there is a right or wrong way to work through your grief. The objective is to start feeling a little better each day.

Denial

The powerful emotion of grief can be too much for many people. Our mind kicks in with a defense mechanism to protect us. Denying the loss allows us to continue as if nothing has happened and we go on as usual. This way of coping helps to numb the intensity of the feelings.

Anger

Some people use anger as a way to hide the other intense feelings they have when someone passes away. Instead of feeling the pain, we get angry, sometimes at ourselves, at objects, or even at the person we have lost. Deep down you know that the person who dies isn't to blame and doesn't deserve your anger but at this stage, your emotions are too strong for your rational brain to have a say.

Bargaining

Loss can bring about feelings of vulnerability and as if we don't have control over some of the major aspects of life. During the bargaining stage, people consider the 'what ifs' in life. By working through the 'what ifs' grievers feel like they can have an impact on the outcomes of an event and therefore take back some of that control.

Depression

Some people in this stage may take a step back, retreat a little and put some space between themselves and the world. Some would call this the quieter stage. The early stages of grief might have involved running from or hiding your feelings but at this point, it is time to start processing them.

Acceptance

There are people who may feel some sense of relief at this stage, that there is a noticeable difference in how they are going about their lives. That being said, one shouldn't confuse acceptance with happiness. This isn't a sign that you have moved on. It does mean that you are now able to see the meaning of this loss in your life and that things are getting better.

Originally, the 5 stages of grief were associated with the loss of a person, but they are also now witnessed with the loss of other things like a job or a relationship. If you have been through any type of breakup or divorce, you can probably easily relate to each of the stages and see how the process of each stage will depend on the relationship.

HOW ARE THE 5 STAGES OF GRIEF RELATED TO TRAUMA

If you go back and look at each of the reasons why we might experience trauma you will notice that each one involves some kind of loss. If you are the victim of sexual abuse or domestic violence you might feel a loss of your sense of self and confidence and certainly a loss of power. Children who have been maltreated or grown up suffering from war trauma may have lost their innocence. Even losing your home, whether because of a divorce or natural disaster, is going to cause grief.

There will be elements of the 5 stages that are relatable to traumatic experiences. A victim of sexual assault may deny it ever happened or play the situation right down. Whatever the type of trauma, it is normal to refuse to accept certain facts. While bargaining, we ponder on all the things we would do to take back the trauma and go back to how things were. Depression after trauma can be mild or severe, you may have the ability to pull yourself from the depression in a few weeks or can take years, like with grief, there are no rules to dictate how and how long this stage lasts. Again, acceptance doesn't mean that the trauma is all done with. You will have reached a point where there will be more good days than bad. Accepting trauma means you know that you can't change the past, but you can make the most of the present.

Anger is the stage that we are most concerned with. If you have lost someone or suffered from acts of violence, a traumatic accident or loss of any kind, one of the things we frequently ask ourselves is "Why me?" or "What have I done to deserve this?". I know I tend to feel angry at the entire world. I felt as if I was being punished but I couldn't understand what I had done to be receiving such an awful experience. I was snappy at everyone and I went from blaming the world to blaming myself and everyone in between.

Anger is a perfectly normal response to trauma. One theory believes that anger fuels us with the energy we need to overcome the challenges in life. Another theory tells us that anger is our response to extreme threats that we have been through during the traumatic experience. We already know that a little bit of anger is ok. But when the problem gets out of hand, it is known as post-traumatic anger.

Post-traumatic anger occurs when the anger from a trauma affects how a person adapts to situations that aren't extremely threatening. A person trying to overcome an act of violence will be suffering from post-traumatic anger if the anger prevents them from being able to continue with their normal daily routines. There are three components. Arousal, often seen in PTSD, is when the heart rate increases, so does the activity in the brain and glandular system in a way that is not considered normal for the level of arousal. For example, a car backfires and the person dives for cover. Our behavior changes as a result of these extreme threats. Some people can become aggressive and others passive aggressive. Our thoughts and beliefs may no longer be the same as before our traumatic experience. It might be easier for you to become angry when people don't follow certain rules, even if you didn't used to follow them. But your focus on potential threats has changed how you think.

HOW TO MOVE ON FROM A TRAUMATIC EXPERIENCE

Whether you have lost a loved one or you have experienced a different kind of trauma, the first thing is to be aware of the 5 stages of grief and recognizing each stage you are in and the depth of that stage. At the same time, recognizing it doesn't mean you need to rush it anyway. Constantly remind yourself that you are allowed to take the time you need to work through your feelings. In the first few weeks or even months, you will probably benefit from some time alone and you need this time to be able to grieve your loss. If you have any doubts about what happened, now is the time to find out. If someone died suddenly, you might want to learn exactly what happened. This will probably hurt, but it will stop you from wondering in the future. If you have been the victim of a crime, it often helps to stay informed about the case and do what you can to bring the criminal to justice. Again, this won't be easy and you might need additional support to find your strength.

Talking will help. It is hard because it means reliving the trauma. You might find talking to friends and family easier because you are more familiar with them, but remember if they haven't experienced the same trauma; they may not be able to help you at first. They may try to offer you advice when all you need is someone to listen to you. This is why joining support groups can be incredibly beneficial. There is a huge amount of comfort talking to those who have been through similar experiences. Doing this reminded me that my feelings were perfectly normal.

For me, writing in a journal was so helpful. A lot of the time I found it hard to talk about my feelings, I didn't want to burden others with what I felt was just me being negative. Writing down how I felt and my experiences throughout each stage allowed me to express myself freely without worrying what others would think. This really helped prepare me to talk to others because I felt more in control of how I expressed myself. It also gave me a chance to look back and reflect on the different stages. When I had days of feeling like there was no progress, I could look back and see just how far I had actually come.

Work on getting yourself back into a routine. Routines offer a sense of security. Getting the right amount of sleep and eating the right foods will provide you with the energy and strength you need to start finding your "normal". It will often be baby steps. Sleep was a particular challenge for me. Personally, I didn't want to take any prescribed medication but that's not to say it isn't the option for you. I found that staying away from caffeine before bed, having a warm bath and practicing mindfulness before going to bed helped getting a better night's sleep. On a bad day, I would listen to podcasts to help me fall asleep. Experts might disagree but it helped my mind stay focused on something other than my pain.

There are a few things that you should also avoid doing:

Don't bottle up your feelings. These are strong emotions that we are going through and keeping them locked inside can make you feel worse in the long run, not to mention the potential damage to your health. If you can't face talking to someone, at least keep a journal.

Don't overdo it. When you start to feel better it's normal to want to become more active as this will help keep your mind active and get back into a routine. Be careful of taking on too much too soon and becoming overwhelmed.

Drugs and alcohol will numb your feelings, but this will only delay you from processing your emotions. They can often lead to other health problems like addiction and depression.

Put off any major life changes. Moving to a new house, changing jobs, etc., are huge changes and right now, you might not be in the right frame of mind to make these decisions.

RECOGNIZING THE NEED FOR PROFESSIONAL HELP

Though I don't like mentioning time frames, we also have to appreciate that there will come a point when you may need professional help, which is perfectly understandable after what you have been through.

If you haven't seen any type of change within 4 to 6 weeks, it might be worth talking to your doctor (GP) for advice on what to do next. Here are some ideas of when you should seek profes- sional help:

- You don't have anyone in your life to talk to. Your
- feelings are too strong for you to cope with. You
- are having suicidal thoughts.
- You experience nightmares and difficulty sleeping.
- Your relationships are suffering.
- Your work is suffering.
- You are dependent on drugs or alcohol.
- You are having accidents.

The following links are for sites that can offer professional help for those who have suffered traumatic experiences.

http://assisttraumacare.org.uk
https://au.reachout.com/mental-health-issues/trauma
https://www.nimh.nih.gov/health/topics/coping-with-traumatic-events/index.shtml

I am truly sorry that you have had to suffer any kind trauma. I'm not going to pretend to know your situation because we all handle things in different ways, but I do know that there is light at the end of the tunnel, and I know that there is nothing wrong with getting help when you need it. Although your situation is unique, there are others who have been through similar experiences and sharing will provide you some relief. Although it may not seem it now, you will be able to start feeling better but it's not something that is just going to pass with time. You need to work through the process, allow yourself time to feel, time to cry, and time to get used to living in a way that allows you to cope. Anger will rise and fall, some days it will be more apparent, stronger, and it will be harder to manage, however you must forgive yourself for this. From here, you can start working on becoming happy again.

6

CHILD TO PARENT VIOLENCE

Domestic violence against women has become a topic that we no longer need to feel ashamed about and there is plenty of help available. Not only that, but laws have changed which help protect violence against women in marriages. In the early 2000s, more studies were carried out regarding domestic abuse against men, something that was even more difficult to admit. It was around the same time that research began on child to parent violence and adolescent to parent violence.

This type of violence is any type of behavior where a child tries to intimidate, threaten, or coerce a parent. It can be physical, verbal, or emotional. And it's more common than you probably know. I wanted to share some statistics so that others can appreciate the extent of the problem.

- Studies over a three-year period in the US showed roughly 6.5% to 10.8% of child to parent violence incidents.
- In Canada, over a 6-month period, physical aggression was at 12% whereas verbal aggression was up to 60%.
- The most in-depth studies were carried out in Spain. The prevalence rate was 21% for physical violence and psychological abuse to 46% for emotional abuse.
- Between 2012 and 2016, there was a 95% increase in cases. Of the 120,051 cases of domestic violence against adults by children investigated, 1,459 young people were charged with offences.
- Over 75% of the time, the mother is the victim.

As the studies are still relatively young, the exact definitions still vary. Some experts include financial abuse, others state that there should be an intent to cause injury, or blackmail.

WHY IS CHILD TO PARENT VIOLENCE SO DIFFICULT TO UNDERSTAND?

If you have children or teenagers, it's not hard to see why the question is rather complicated to answer. Even if you don't have children, you can still look back on your youth and probably remember some occasions where your behavior would now be considered abusive.

The transition from baby to toddler, toddler to child and child to teenager presents gigantic learning stages when it comes to emotions. Toddlers become angry as they might not have the vocabulary to express their emotions, children are learning about these emotions as their interactions with the world and new people grow. Your once little person who needed their mum for comfort and support has now been injected with a rush of hormones and it can feel like you hardly know who they are anymore. Anger is a part of these rites of passage. Like all humans, they have the right to explore their emotions and learn how to express them the right way. Each stage, these young people are learning about boundaries and what limits there are in the world while also learning how to set their own boundaries. They are testing the power of balance.

So, the question is, how do you know when there is a problem. When does your child or teenager go from expressing healthy anger as part of learning to taking over the power in the relationship?

The other side of the problem is that it is very difficult for parents to admit that there is a problem. Despite blaming ourselves in cases of domestic abuse, once we move past denial, we know that it was the person who was abusive that is to blame. With our children, it is never going to be quite so black and white. We raised these people, we instilled our beliefs and values, we taught them right from wrong and we hope that we have set the right example for them. Being on the receiving end of child violence can be shameful and disappointing.

WHY DO TEENAGERS FEEL ANGRY?

In many cases, teenagers feel angry for the same reason that we do. While they don't have the pressure of balancing work and home, or the financial strain adults might find themselves under, they still have a lot of stress to manage. The relationships that we form throughout high school are incredibly volatile, yet we are sure they are going to last forever, be that romantic or friendships. Any slight upset to these relationships can cause a teenager to feel angry. At the same time, there is pressure to do well academically, and they are still learning how to be autonomous and manage their own time so that everything gets done and there is still time to enjoy themselves. Let's look at some other possible causes of child to parent violence:

- An argument with a parent getting out of control.
- The inability to handle their own problems which causes frustration.

- A lack of respect for their parents or a lack of consequences for their actions.
- Fighting back from abuse from their parents, whether physical or emotional.
- Revenge for something parents have done.
- Mental illness or not being able to handle family members with a mental illness.
- Drug or alcohol abuse or exposure to gang culture.

I always try and think of the range of things that can make me angry and then consider the additional years I have had to learn how to manage these situations. Remember, empathy isn't the same as forgiveness, but it can give you the chance to see things from their point of view and to learn more about what makes them angry. The hope is that being a role model in this way will help your child to be more empathetic towards your feelings.

WHAT ARE THE SIGNS OF CHILD TO ADULT VIOLENCE

Visible abuse is easier to spot. Hitting, punching, kicking, shoving, hair pulling, spitting, and throwing things are all considered abusive. Some of the psychological behaviors are harder as it is difficult to separate them from everyday teenage behavior. Some examples include:

- Name-calling
- Criticism
- Refusing to do as they are told
- Being late despite being aware of curfews
- Skipping school
- Stealing or demanding things that aren't affordable
- Creating fear in the home
- Running away or threatening to
- Threatening to hurt a parent or themselves (self-harm)

One of the hardest decisions you may have to make is figuring out whether your child genuinely is a risk to their own safety or yours, or whether it is a cry out for attention. Either situation will be a cause for concern and should never be taken lightly. Even young people who seem to have empty threats are likely to have underlying issues. Like anger, self-harming is a way of trying to cope with intense emotions and distress. Your instincts will probably tell you what is normal teenage anger and what isn't, but self-harm can lead to more serious issues and it is more difficult to spot.

Signs of self-harm can include dramatic changes in sleeping, eating or mood, there might be a drop in school performance or a lack of interest to do things with friends, all of which can be easily mistaken for the usual "teenage behavior". There may also be injuries that your child can't explain. Another difficult sign is when a child avoids showing parts of their body where unexplainable injuries occur, but again, you might put this down to changes in their body that they would prefer not to show.

As a parent, I know how hard it is to bring up difficult conversations with children and more so teenagers. Before we even open our mouths, we fear the response. Regardless of how smart we are, from the point of view of our teenagers, we know nothing about how difficult their lives are. Even those who have the closest of relationships with their children will come to a point where they question where this relationship has suddenly gone.

Self-harm can't be overlooked. Cuts can lead to infections and the problem can quickly escalate into something more dangerous. It is crucial that you talk to your child in a non-judgmental way. Make sure they know there are people they can talk to, whether that's you, another family member, or a professional. It's not exactly a form of child to parent abuse but it's still going to stir up feelings of guilt, shame and fear and you will feel great pain watching your child suffer. Don't forget the importance of looking after yourself if you are coping with a child or teenager who self-harms, you need your strength and well-being. For help with taking care of yourself, you will be able to find plenty of techniques in Chapter 9.

WHAT CAUSES CHILDREN TO BE VIOLENT TOWARDS THEIR PARENTS?

It's wrong to assume that a violent or abusive child has been exposed to some form of violence or abuse in the past. It is certainly possible, but there are also children who are violent to parents who are kind, loving, and supportive, and who have never raised a hand to their child. By assuming violence comes from violence makes it very hard some parents to come to terms with the problem. It's perfectly normal for families to refuse to see the situation for what it is because there has never been any violence in the home. Research is still young in this field, but it may also be caused by mental health issues or attachment difficulties. Don't fall for the theory of exposure to violence just because our lack of understanding makes this idea the society norm or comfortable. The causes are complex and one of the principal reasons for getting professional help is because they are probably more intricate than we would imagine.

HELP FOR CHILD TO PARENT VIOLENCE

Regardless of whether your family unit is just the two of you or there are two parents and more siblings, child to parent violence can impact the whole family. We are going to look at what you can do to make sure you are taking care of yourself so that you are better able to help your child.

How to Take Care of Your Needs

So much emotional turmoil is almost impossible to escape and the stress and negative emotions will consume you, eventually, this will have consequences on your own health, especially if you don't look after yourself.

For your emotional health, you need to know that this isn't your fault. Despite being responsible for the upbringing of this person, there are some things out of your control, and you can't feel guilty or question what you have done wrong. Society and culture can have a strong influence on our young people or there could be underlying mental health issues. Don't beat yourself up or question your parenting.

On a similar note, I have to mention what could be seen as holding parents at ransom. I was talking to a parenting group some time ago and I listened to one mum tell her story. Her child had mental health issues but was using this to his advantage, almost as if manipulating his mum. He was refusing to go to school, he ate when he wanted and wouldn't join the daily at mealtimes and all sorts of other behaviors which were crushing the mom's soul. In this situation, the balance of power and respect had been lost but the mum saw know way of restoring it because each time she tried to assert herself, the child used his mental health as an excuse, like a get out of jail free card. Needless to say, that this isn't always the case, but this type of abuse is also more common than we realize and leads us to doubt our parenting.

No one is a perfect parent, and we all learn as we are going. Looking back over the years and analyzing every parenting decision you made isn't going to help you, it is more likely to exhaust you. We need to focus on being the best parent possible now.

From now on, it's about recognizing that there is a problem. Your instincts have probably been trying to tell you this, but you have been pushing it down and thinking its normal behavior or that it's a phase they will grow out of. I found this was almost a relief. Before, it felt as if there was no end to the problem or that it was only going to keep getting worse. Deciding that this was the time to make a change gave me strength.

As with adult anger, there will be a root of your child's anger and we need to uncover what this is. So, you might need to re-educate yourself on the foundations of communication. Successful communication is 40% talking and 60% listening. Regardless of who we are talking to, we often feel the need to jump in with solutions but more often than not, the person just wants us to listen, and allow them to get everything off their chest without interruptions. Sit facing your child and give them all of your attention. Make sure other siblings who may want your attention aren't around and it goes without saying, leave your phone in another room. It's a good idea to reflect what they are saying so they know that you are actively listening, for example, "So, you are feeling angry because your teachers don't listen to you". Don't feel the need to give unrequested advice.

Because children and teenagers are still working on their communication skills, it's essential that you lead by example. If you can teach them how to listen it will make it easier when you need to explain how the violent and abusive behavior won't be tolerated anymore. Explain your boundaries clearly, without raising your voice or becoming emotional. When you are thinking about what is tolerable and what isn't, you should also consider which battles are worth the fight. Take a single mum as an example, they will have to fight every battle with their child, and this is a horrible role to have to take on. Trying to change too many of your child's behaviors at once can lead to further resistance. Start on the things that you absolutely won't put up with.

As hard as it is, you will have to be consistent with your boundaries. There is little point in making great progress with open communication only for them to know that these were empty promises. If you have told your child that you will call the police after any physical violence, you must do it, so they know that your boundaries won't be crossed. This is how you are going to keep yourself safe. On the other hand, if you have made a promise to your child, it is absolutely essential that you keep it.

If you struggle to even have a conversation with your child, you can suggest that together, you find a professional that they can talk to. Because of the stigma of "speaking to a shrink", your child might not welcome the idea. Rather than making this another battle to fight, make sure that you find someone that you can talk to and provide you with support.

There is another balance to find, and that is the amount of time that you spend with your child. As tempted as you are to spend every minute with them, you are going to risk suffocating them. We all need a certain amount of space and it will also help to show that you trust them. The time you spend with them needs to be productive. Suggest going for walks or watching films together. See if there is a new hobby that they would like to start, perhaps even something that can be used as an outlet for their anger. Make some time for yourself too. Don't abandon who you are and what you love doing because you think you need to be with your child, because that isn't balanced.

Finally, remember that your child and behavior are two separate entities. Your child's behavior is bad, they aren't. You need to make sure that your actions and the language you use reflects this. Your child needs to know that you love them, and you can see that they are still a good person and that it is their behavior that needs to change, not them as a person.

Doesn't it all sound so simple on paper! There is one thing that I have always said and that is being a parent is the best but most difficult job in the world. Nobody wants their children to grow up too quickly but many times I have thought "Just wait till you are a mom and you will see how hard this is". All we want to do is be their friend and while that's a beautiful concept, it's impractical. Children and teenagers have friends. What they need from us is an example and a strong set out boundaries and guidelines that will set them up to be a good adult. And for this, they need parents.

HOW TO HELP TEENAGERS MANAGE THEIR ANGER

Throughout this chapter, we have already looked at some ways that will help your child or teenager manage their anger. Let's recap them quickly:

- Work on health communication with them so they know that they can talk to you without being judged or reprimanded. Actively listen to the person and appreciate what they are saying and allow them to talk about their emotions.
- Make time for them. Do things that you both enjoy doing.
- Get to the root of their anger either through talking to them or buy noticing any patterns.
- Find outlets for their anger. This will vary from one person to the next. Some might want to take part in sports, arts and crafts, music, yoga, or meditation. Put forward some suggestions and see which gets the most enthusiastic response. Don't give up if they don't like something, keep going until you find something.
- Set boundaries and teach your child how to set boundaries. While you expect your child to respect

your boundaries, you need to be able to do the same.
- Get professional help for your child when necessary or if you are unsure, talk to your doctor.

Here are 10 other techniques that will help your child manage their anger:

1. Manage your anger

One of the greatest motivations I had to manage my own anger was because I knew that my children were following in my unhealthy anger steps. It's not fair to expect your child to manage their anger when you aren't doing the same. You can even talk about your anger management and the coping techniques with your older children so they understand that instead of being ashamed of it, you can work on it together.

2. Teach family members self-directed time-outs.

Time-outs aren't a punishment and it's not the same as the naughty step for little children. Time-outs allow family members space when a situation becomes heated. Instead of things spiraling out of control, teach people to walk away from 10 to 15 minutes so that everyone can calm down. Once everyone has a chance to compose themselves, you can return to the issue at hand. Just remember that it's important not to use time-outs as a way of ignoring problems.

3. Teach your children to be problem-solvers

We can all think back to a moment when we became angry because we couldn't fix or do something. Giving children the ability to solve their own problems isn't only going to help them manage their anger, it's also a valuable life skill. When problems arise, look at three or four potential solutions together. Ask them what the advantages and disadvantages of each could be and encourage them to make their own decision. If things don't go to plan, it's just as important to encourage them. Again, we have tried things that haven't worked out and we have to go to 'Plan B', seriously, there is nothing wrong with this and our children need to know this.

4. Understand the stress that your child is under

Ok, it's not the same as the stress you have but then again, they don't have the years that you have, so it's important to put this in perspective. 3 exams, an argument with a friend, and acne to a teenager can be equal to your work stress, an argument with your partner and that backache that won't go away. I have done this myself and regretted it. My teenager complains about too much homework while I'm doing the ironing at 11 o'clock at night. If only homework was my only problem. Belittling their problems won't help when it comes to encouraging them to open up about what worries them or makes them angry. And yes, on the scale of things, their problems have easier solutions, but this is the beauty of age and wisdom.

5. Keep things much shorter and much simpler

This piece of advice was like magic to me. Your child asks you for something and you know you have to say no. But you feel the need to come up with a lengthy explanation to justify your no. But they don't have the attention span or inclination to listen to this, so while you think you are doing a good job, your child may not hear more than the no! Look at the two following examples:

- *Mom, can I meet my friends tonight?*
- I don't think it's a good idea because I know you haven't finished your homework, plus, your bedroom is a state and I wanted to watch this documentary with you. It's nearly the weekend so you can make plans once all your jobs are done.
- *Mom, can I meet my friends tonight?*
- No, you know the rules.
- *Mom, can I meet my friends tonight?*
- Yes, you have done a great job on your homework and thank you for keeping your room tidy.

In the first example, teenagers hear "I don't think" and they are unlikely to listen to the rest. For them, it's a no, and they are angry. You have a better chance of getting your message across if it is short.

6. Decide when your no is negotiable

Don't confuse this one with your boundaries. Boundaries are non-negotiable! There are some situations where you may have what I call a "weak no". But before we go any further, the weakness is only visible to you. If there is something your child wants, and may become angry if they don't get it, think about it. If your child doesn't want to eat the same dinner as the rest of the family, it's easy for this situation to become an angry one. From your point of view, you are too exhausted to cook and clean up after two meals. But what if they could cook and clean up after making their own dinner. Doesn't it benefit both of you to negotiate?

I know I have said this before, but I really do want you to understand that I have tried all of these options and learnt from my mistakes. So, from my personal experience, my teenager refused to eat what I had cooked. I told her to cook her own dinner and I was so happy that she asked for my opinion on herbs, spices, etc. Her dinner was delicious, and it encouraged her to make it for the rest of the family at least once a week.

This was such a help to understand what I could negotiate on. Giving children, particularly teenagers, the option to decide whether they accept a no or can find an alternative is an amazing way to eliminate anger and you actually get to feel like a genuinely good parent.

7. Be careful not to react to passive-aggressive behavior

Passive-aggressive behavior is a form of manipulation. If you ask your child to do something and they do it in a way that is intended to annoy you, by reacting, they win. If you ask your child to tidy their bedroom and they put their music on full blast, you are going to get angry— that's the point! If you don't react, they will quickly learn that passive -aggressive behavior doesn't work.

8. Find Humor

Yes, there are ways to still laugh with your child. It may have to be at yourself, but there are also a massive range of things that you can just take a moment together to laugh at. YouTube has so many examples. Tell them about those blunders you make during the day that you are probably embarrassed about. In those difficult years, the best gift is when you can both laugh so much you cry.

9. Show them your love

The older our children get, the harder it seems to be to show our love. Those hugs from the pre-teen years just don't seem to be enough. This doesn't mean you have to go out and buy the latest trends. Buy their favorite food, make their bed for them once in a while, give them a hug, text them with the latest trendy emoji, leave them notes, show them their baby books. Nine times out of ten you will be met with "that's so sad", but like you when you were that age, they will appreciate it.

10. Respect your children

Treating people how you wish to be treated is something many seem to have forgotten. Be kind and caring to your children so they know that these are important family values. Respect their wishes and their feelings if you hope to be treated the same way.

I can't say it enough, there are jobs in the world that seem difficult. Prime ministers and presidents have so much responsibility, CEOs, and managers, they all have a lot on their plate. But when it comes to your children, there is no greater responsibility in the world. It might seem like you can't get it right, but I promise that you can. More often than not we are so involved that we can't see the woods (or the forest) for the trees. We are so involved that the bigger picture is impossible to imagine.

Take that necessary step back so that you have the chance to see things more clearly. Don't be scared to walk away knowing that you will be better prepared to handle the situation once you have had time to yourself. There are situations that you will be able to handle yourself and others that will require professional help. Neither one means you have failed nor that you are a bad parent. Don't look at other families and think that they have it all under control. You never know what happens behind closed doors and it has no reflection on your family or the way you bring up your children.

I have offered the best advice I can with regards to child to parent violence, but it is still a very individual situation. From personal experience, you do everything you can and when you can put your hand on your heart and say you have tried everything, you seek professional help. Never forget that child to parent violence is still relatively new, so finding help is the logical thing to do.

7

ANGER AND OUR PHYSICAL HEALTH

Nobody wants to read a book that is just too repetitive so I will briefly review some of the physical health impacts of anger so you don't have to go back and find them again before we move on to some of the other ways anger can take its toll on our bodies.

When anger is left unmanaged, it can have a number of short and long-term consequences on our health. This can include:

- Headaches or migraines,
- Stomachaches and other digestive problems
- Skin problems such as ache, eczema, or psoriasis
- High blood pressure
- Insomnia

- Anxiety and depression
- Heart attacks and/or strokes

This is what the scientists say and it's certainly true. But how about we take it out of the textbook analogy and really look at what anger does to us. What I am about to describe is based on my experiences, however, I'm sure you will be able to relate.

In those incredibly intense moments of anger, I can't breathe. My lungs physically hurt, and I feel as if I can't take in enough oxygen. I have suffered from panic attacks, so I am now able to control the anger enough so that it doesn't get that far but I still notice that pain in my chest if I am not careful.

When I was younger, I used to think that when people said, "with a heavy heart", they were just being poetic. During my battles with anger, I can appreciate where the expression comes from. To me, it's like those old-style scales where you need to add more weights to get the right balance- The problem was that all the weights were pulling my heart down and there was nothing on the other end to balance it out.

Then, there is the insomnia. I'm not a negative person. In fact, despite all that life has thrown at me, I am proud to say that people praise my positivity. That being said, not even my positivity was strong enough to win the internal battle. I would tell myself that I was going to go to bed and have a good night's sleep and the world would be a better place the next day. After 10 minutes of my brain replaying situations, I would become more and more angry until I had to get up.

Everyone has these moments at some point in their life. It's not until you start going through the same thing day in and day out that you begin to see the impact on your well-being. I had become almost gray in complexion, my hair was lifeless, and I began to notice more, let's call them "silver highlights". And this was only what I could see. It was hard to imagine what this horrible anger was doing to my insides. The realization that anger was not only ruining my life but also shortening it was a hard truth to face.

And even though I was aware of what was happening, this didn't wake me up and tell me that I needed to change. It scared me! It made me more nervous. Situations that already brought about anxiety were now terrifying. Moments of anxiety became longer and more of a challenge to overcome. I started getting sick, every bug or virus and you could guarantee I would get it.

HOW ANGER AFFECTS US PHYSICALLY

As we have seen, the brain is an amazing organ and I'm convinced we don't take care of it well enough. Becoming angry triggers, a series of processes that can explain why we don't always make the right decisions and harms our memory. Let's take a closer look at how.

1. Before we are even aware of what is happening, anger reaches our amygdala (a collection of cells associated with our emotional memory).
2. The amygdala then kicks the hypothalamus into action. The nervous system and the endocrine system are connected via the hypothalamus.
3. The hypothalamus creates CRH- corticotrophin releasing hormone (a hormone that affects how we cope with stress, depression, etc.). CRH activates the pituitary glands.
4. Here, the pituitary creates ACTH- adrenocorticotropic hormone, which is necessary for your adrenal glands to function properly.
5. Now, moving away from your brain to the adrenal glands (just above your kidneys), stress hormones like cortisol, adrenaline and noradrenaline are produced.

YASMIN A.

It is the increased level of cortisol that interests us at this point. This overload of cortisol means that our neurons are taking in too much calcium and can encourage cells to fire too often and die. A loss of neurons has two serious implications, one on the Prefrontal cortex and the other on the hippocampus.

When we start to lose neurons in the prefrontal cortex, we struggle to make the best decisions, our judgement is impaired, and it's difficult to plan well for the future. The effect on the hippocampus is that our short-term memory starts to weaken. Have you ever had a moment when you have walked away from an argument or situation and then thought of the right words to say? We struggle to remember what we want to say at the time because of the strain on our short-term memory. It also makes it more difficult to create new memories.

Finally, with too much cortisol in our body, our serotonin levels drop. This happy hormone can prevent us from feeling anger more intensely, it reduces the chance of us becoming aggressive, and can lower the risk of depression.

While we are on the subject of hormones, premenstrual syndrome (PMS), or menstrual rage is another common cause of mood swings and anger. The drop in estrogen and progesterone during ovulation influences the serotonin in your body. Due to the intricate nature of our bodies and hormones, you will be able to find out more about this in my next book, which will be dedicated to the dreaded 'M' word–menopause!

OUR PHYSICAL HEALTH AND RELATIONSHIPS

Whether it's your own anger or your partner, there is going to be a negative impact on this relationship. It is also common for the other person to respond in anger, making the whole situation worse and the relationship just becomes an angry one. When this starts to happen, you will end up feeling angry more frequently and your anger will last for longer, so the physical symptoms we mentioned before are exasperated.

Often when we are in a long-term relationship, we fall into the assumption that your partner should know how you are feeling. Our anger can be a result of lacking the ability to express other concerns we might have. It becomes frustrating when they can't see how you really feel after all this time together. But they aren't mind readers and need help in understanding the underlying problems.

We have learnt that in some cases, angry bursts can be good. They can clear the air and give the other person a chance to see things that they may not have seen before. On the other hand, there are other ways in which our anger manifests in a relationship.

- **Snapping-** rapid responses that warn a person they are pushing your limits. It might not cause a partner to immediately respond with anger but if it continues, they probably will.
- **Nitpicking-** This can come across as nagging, reminding the other person of things they haven't done or the things they do wrong. It can also be sarcasm. Nitpicking leads to distance.
- **Explosions-** it might be just that one thing they have done, the icing on the cake, and there is an explosion of anger, insults, and the need to win while rarely letting the partner speak.
- **The silent treatment-** sometimes we think that the silent treatment is the safest option as it stops us from saying what we want. A partner may feel like they must give in to any request in order to end the icy atmosphere.
- **Escaping-** when anger becomes too much we withdraw from the situation and turn too much of our attention to something else. It could be work or hobbies, anything to stay away from the home. Some people will turn to drugs or alcohol as a way to escape.

- **Backup-** bringing in other people or even just the opinions of others to bring in more power to the argument.

Regardless of which anger style you or your partner has, the physical consequences will be the same. We are putting our mental and physical health at great risk, especially if it continues for longer periods of time.

You may also find that the longer this anger between you continues, the harder it is to put things right. It seems to be the new normal or you forget why you fell in love in the first place and fear that the only solution is to call it a day.

Communication is the key to fixing this wrong. It also means that you may have to understand that there is a difficult conversation to be had. In the first place, you need to find the right moment, when you are both calm and relaxed and there aren't a million other things to do.

It's important not to blame your partner for the anger in the relationship. That being said, neither should you take all the responsibility. This conversation shouldn't be a blame game but a proactive way to find solutions. Use "I" statements to avoid making the other person feel like the problems are their fault. For example, I feel hurt when you aren't interested in my day".

Remember that it's not just about you and they need to have the opportunity to express how they are feeling. If they aren't forthcoming, ask questions to try and encourage them. Genuinely listen to what they are saying because there will be changes you can make to improve the situation too; even small changes can make a big difference.

Try not to only focus on the negatives. There are probably still some positives that you can talk about that will remind you both that all is not lost. This will help to keep you both in a good place mentally and stop anger from making an appearance, which in turn will help you to come up with some solutions.

BREAKING THE ANGER CYCLE

There is no need to tell you that anger is a vicious cycle. It begins with your trigger, let's say your partner has forgotten to get the washing in and now it's raining. This causes a negative thought, "He is so selfish and unable to think of anything that's not related to him". Next comes your emotional response, you are angry and frustrated because you are going to have to redo the washing. Your body then reacts, increased heart rate, gritted teeth, and finally, your behavioral response is to shout at your partner. They may respond with a comment that causes another trigger and the cycle begins again.

At some point we have to learn how to break this cycle, not only for your relationship, but also for your physical and mental health.

USING RATIONAL BEHAVIOR TO BREAK THE ANGER CYCLE

Being rational means taking a logical and sensible perspective. It's not always easy when anger seems to have control over us and so being self-aware is really going to help. When we are self-aware, we are able to spot each step in the anger cycle and take measures to break it.

This is why one of the most valuable techniques in anger management is taking a step back. Telling your brain to just stop for a minute. This pause enables you to see things from a different point of view. Maybe your partner was busy with the kids or got home late from work. Perhaps they genuinely forgot. The trigger will always be there, and most likely, so will the negative thought. However, if we can take that crucial moment to counteract the negative thought with a logical explanation, we are more likely to prevent the emotional and behavioral responses, as well as the physical symptoms anger causes.

YASMIN A.

HELPING OTHERS BREAK THEIR ANGER CYCLE

Really, we can only control our own emotions and it is down to our partner to control theirs. Nevertheless, as a partnership, sometimes it works to your advantage when you help each other out with anger management.

Once you have seen the benefit of stopping and taking a step back to reevaluate the situation, you will notice that arguments tend not to spiral out of control so much. I also find that it is good just to say "Stop". When you are both angry and you can feel that it is only going to get worse say it, don't shout it. Explain that you both need a minute. Put your hand on their arm or their hand so they know you aren't being aggressive. Don't walk away, just pause and breathe. Even a minute or two is enough for both of you to think more sensibly.

As part of my anger management, I used the science to help me take that moment. Counting to 10 didn't seem to work for me in every situation so I needed a new technique to focus my mind and become calm again. When I experienced a trigger, I would imagine how my brain responds. I would tell myself that now we are at the amygdala, and I would imagine this flow of energy to the hypothalamus. I would visualize the hormones being created and firing around my body. On the bad days, I would have a troop of serotonin soldiers who would jump into action and start fighting their way back to victory. It might sound silly, but it is important to find a technique that works for you so that you are able to block the chain of events. This leads us nicely into the next chapter where we will look at more ways to train our brains.

8

TRAIN YOUR BRAIN TO CHANGE THE OUTCOMES

With absolutely no disrespect to other anger management books (because I have read a great number of them), I took all of what was useful to me and then adapted it. Because anger, and life in general is still so different for men and women, there was a lot of advice and information that was general but the only way I can explain it is that it didn't really hit the spot. I knew I had to change how my brain was working but the practical and the theory can't be the same for the different sexes, simply because everything from our brains to our day is different.

The point is that while we know that techniques like deep breathing and counting to ten really do help in a number of situations, but this chapter is going to be dedicated to solutions that are more related to training our brains to change the outcomes. I want to look at alternative techniques that help women who need a long-term solution to anger management.

WHAT DOES A HEALTHY BRAIN LOOK LIKE?

Don't worry, this is not a scientific question that identifies the physical signs of a healthy brain. My mental image is slightly pink and cushiony, so we will stick to that. We will consider a healthy brain as one that functions in our favor. The following list is an idea of the signs of a healthy brain. Please don't panic if you don't tick off everyone. Even with anger management, we can have moments when we don't feel like our brain is the most perfectly functioning organ!

- You have a calm mind - you are able to handle your stress and you do yoga, meditation, or proactive mindfulness so that you are able to enjoy a greater sense of calm. For some, it's not necessary to stick to these practices but the benefits far outweigh the time you spend doing so. You may have other stress outlets that make you feel calm.
- You are able to let things go - holding onto things encourages you to rethink situations over and over again. It's a massive topic so we will focus on this in the next chapter.

YASMIN A.

- You feel that your emotions are under control- not just the negative emotions, but all of them. We need to be fully aware of our highs and lows and know how to control them.
- You can sleep- I'm not talking about sleeping in until the late hours. It's about getting the right number of hours and the right quality of sleep. So many times, I have gone to bed early yet still woken up tired because despite the hours, the sleep was disturbed.
- You have physical balance- it might be something simple like losing your footing, tripping upstairs, or you can't quite master that yoga pose. Strong balance requires mental fitness and a healthy brain.
- Your long-term and short-term memory are both 'there'- it's impossible to remember everything and don't put pressure on yourself to do so. We have lists and photo albums for a good reason—they jog the memory. However, there is cause for concern when your memory fails you too often.
- You don't struggle to make decisions- a healthy brain is able to rely on good instincts that you use to make decisions.
- You exercise- people who are active, fit and not overweight have healthier brains. Research has shown

that obesity increases the risk of brain shrinkage. Even 10 minutes of walking a day improves the brain and further research suggests that people who walk fast have enhanced memory and a larger brain.
- You spend time with your friends - spending time with friends and enjoying yourself increases oxytocin which reduces cortisol, helping to improve your mood.

We have looked at different methods for anger management that have mainly focused on anger in that moment, for example, how we break the cycle of anger, taking deep breaths or visualization. We saw how emotionally intelligent people question their feelings, look for secondary emotions, and learn to empathize. These are all marvelous ways to control your anger. Now let's look at what we can do to turn our anger into peace and happiness.

TECHNIQUES TO TRAIN THE BRAIN

The key word we have to focus on is 'train'. It's unlikely that you will be able to read the following suggestions and master them straight away. The brain is a powerful tool and may resist at first, after all, it has spent a long time in a state of anger and change takes a little time. Don't give up because you will start to notice a difference and probably sooner than you think.

A counterintuitive exercise

In this exercise we create a link or a connection to anger with love. The person or situation that has caused you to become angry, may not make you feel love, but more often than not, you do still love them. When your kids or your partner make you angry, repeat "I love them". This will help to train your brain to feel love when anger arises.

Use anger to make you stronger

Even though you don't always feel it, you are a strong person. It just might take a little brain training to see this. Focus on what it is that makes you angry and use this to create an empowering plan. Perhaps you need some new knowledge or skills that help you to fight and beat your anger. Even small steps towards becoming stronger will do wonders for your confidence.

Detachment

Imagine yourself separating from the anger and the situation. There will be negative, neutral, and although harder to see, there will still be some positive aspects. Resist focusing on what is negative. Ignore what is neutral. Choose to see the positive.

The loving-kindness method

Also known as Metta practice, this is a type of short meditation when you mental send well-wishes to other people, in our case, those who trigger our anger. If someone recklessly overtakes you while driving too fast, hope that they don't have an accident and that they arrive wherever they need to be in one piece and on time.

Find your comforting object

This could be your pet, a favorite keepsake from your childhood, a stress ball, or it could be a comforting action like running your fingers through your hair. We all probably have one thing that brings us an instant sense of peace. Find it and use it, always keep it nearby for boosts of tranquility and joy.

An alternative use of the deep breath

We commonly use this when we feel like an angry explosion is about to occur, but it can also be used throughout the day for smaller triggers. When you start to take a deep breath for any annoying little occurrences throughout the day, you are training your brain to react to your triggers with a deep breath. It almost becomes an unconscious action.

YASMIN A.

Find your happy song

I know this sounds trivial with a big issue like anger but remember we are looking for solutions that will make us happier and more at peace. Music has immense power on our mood. Whether it's the latest song from your favorite artist or an old classic, play your song. Play it loud, sing and dance. Enjoy the complete experience. If you can't listen to it in the moment, close your eyes and put yourself in the front row of the concert.

Create a happiness handbook

I admit that this might sound a little cheesy but as soon as you start using it, you will feel the benefits. This could be a happiness handbook or a happiness sheet, as long as it is small enough to be able to take around with you. Write, draw, cut, and stick images into your book or onto your page. A personal tip here, don't use things that you think you should include. Naturally, you should have your children, but I tried this and after an argument, looking at my happiness sheet and their photos just made me feel worse. I learnt that green landscapes, wild horses, and images of rainbows gave me a sense of peace and put a smile on my face. When in need, take it out and gaze over your positivity.

The next set of techniques are related more to control than to converting anger into peace. Nevertheless, they are still invaluable techniques.

HOW MUCH CONTROL DO WE REALLY HAVE?

Honestly, this section challenged me! I researched the scientific studies related to emotional and cognitive control, as well as other forms of self-control. All the theories made perfect sense, but it all fell under the category of "it's easier said than done" in our situation.

For example, attention control - our ability to choose what we pay attention to and what we ignore. I want to ignore my family leaving their shoes all over the house and though now, I am better at not getting into a fit of rage about it, I struggle to see why I should ignore this behavior. Reasoning is another, but can we reason with a teenager when both parties are angry?

As you would assume, the answer is yes. Psychologists have dedicated their whole careers on self-control and their research has been of tremendous help in the field of psychology and anger management. But can we really just say that our anger is a question of our control?

Self-control is "the ability to delay gratification, resisting short-term temptation in order to meet long-term goals". My problem here is that anger is not gratifying and why we all want to reach our objectives, there is no temptation to get angry. Let's look at one of the most famous studies regarding self-control and delayed gratification- the Marshmallow Test.

WHAT IS THE MARSHMALLOW TEST?

The Marshmallow Test is when you put a marshmallow in front of a child and tell them that if they don't eat it, in 15 minutes they will have two to eat. The adult then leaves the room. They have to apply self-control if they want to gain more. The same theory can be applied to practically everything, so my goal became understanding how this self-control can benefit those who suffer with anger. The Marshmallow test has been carried out in numerous situations and here are some of the findings

The Marshmallow Test showed that:

- Those who waited longer have different activity in the prefrontal cortex and they were better at pursuing long-term goals.
- Adults were found to have lower BMI (body mass index) and were less prone to drug use.

- We all have choices, but it's our ability to control ourselves that determines the outcome.
- Children who repeated the Marshmallow Test learnt and were able to wait for longer.

This final point is what filled me with positivity. That we do learn. That one positive experience, regardless of whether it is just a marshmallow, can teach our brain to continue and get better.

When I was at my lowest, I remember someone telling me that I needed to see the positive in life. They meant no harm and it is true. But imagine the same advice for someone who is contemplating suicide, how can you tell them that they have reason to be positive if they are breathing. Or that there are people in the world that love you when you experience nothing but hatred and anger.

Training your brain to see the beauty in life and the positives is a journey. We aren't going to climb Everest without first deciding that we want to. So before jumping to look for the good in life, decide that you want to. Then you can make your plan for this scary yet amazing journey. Making this crucial decision to change is the first of many small steps, but this decision is completely under your control. The joy of making this decision will empower you to take further small steps.

YASMIN A.

MY BIG MARSHMALLOW TIP

To fully appreciate the power of your own self-control, I recommend adapting the Marshmallow Test to you. On Monday, put something on or in your fridge, it must be something you want. Some examples could be a $20 note or your favorite box of chocolates. In a cupboard (out of sight) put two $20 notes or two boxes of chocolate. After one week of looking at your "treat" and resisting, enjoy the reward of double. Don't pay the bills with your money or feel guilty because of your diet— allow your brain to enjoy the reward.

Nothing mentioned above appears overly complicated to do, nevertheless, when life is getting us down and it is hard to see the light, it's difficult to imagine something so simple having such an impact. The problem is we may try these techniques once or twice and convince ourselves that they aren't going to work.

For years I have been trying to decorate my desserts with amazing caramel cones and nests but for the life of me, I still haven't got there. I will use my stubbornness to my advantage, and I know that I will learn. Like your strength, use stubbornness and determination to continue with these techniques. It's true that not all will work for everyone, so take the techniques you like, adapt them to suit your needs and personality.

Creating calm and control isn't something that everyone can do alone. Anger issues and continuous stress might be so overwhelming that the brain is unable to take this step back and to learn how to relax. If you have tried the techniques and you aren't seeing the results that you had hoped, it is probably time to find help. This could be in the form of psychotherapy or even just joining a yoga class that will help you to learn how to meditate in the correct way. Meditation and mindfulness aren't just about sitting down and emptying your mind. It takes training, awareness, and a great deal of focus. Yoga experts know how to create the right environment to help you achieve this. Reach out if you need to because trust me, you won't be alone.

9

LEARNING TO FORGIVE AND SEEKING FORGIVENESS

In this chapter we are going to look at three things that will help you along your journey of changing anger into peace and happiness, which will become the new norm. These things are forgiveness, guilt, and the power of an apology.

Mistakes are frequent and no one is safe from them. It might be something silly like burning the dinner (because you were rushing around doing 5 other things) or something more serious like getting angry and hurting someone's feelings. First, we are going to take a look at why and how to forgive ourselves for the mistakes we make.

6 STEPS TO FORGIVING OURSELVES

Learning to forgive ourselves is what will help us to let go of the heavy weight we are carrying on our shoulders. All the pain and sadness that sits on our mind will only start to lessen when we can stop beating ourselves up for our past mistakes. Forgiveness isn't the same as forgetting or giving yourself a free pass. These emotions still need to be processed and so the beginning of forgiveness starts with recognizing the emotions that arise when you make a mistake. Why don't we stick to the burnt dinner? I'm hoping I'm not alone on this one, and look at the stages involved.

1. **Acknowledge your feelings** - I have burnt the dinner and I feel stupid as it is something, I make every week and I should know better. I am also angry because now it means I have to waste time cooking another meal and the whole evening is going to run late.
2. **Admit your mistake** - This is hard because if others had helped me, I could have focused on the dinner. Nevertheless, I have to take responsibility for my actions, and I should have managed my time better. Say it loud and clear so that it becomes real "I burnt the dinner". Not "I burnt the dinner

because nobody helps me" as this is shifting the blame.

3. **Allow yourself a pause** - I'm going to choose to put my mistake and my emotions in a temporary mental box. This is because I still have the usual evening chores to get through plus another dinner to cook. I can't process things properly right now as I will get in a mental muddle.

4. **Readdressing the mistake** - Everyone is fed, the dishes are done, and we are organized for the following day. Because the situation was handled, there is no need for me to feel so self-critical. I successfully solved the problem and there were no serious consequences.

5. **The lesson** - What have I learnt from this mistake? I know that while nobody is going to offer to help, I could ask for it. Somebody else could be tidying up and getting the washing in so that I can at least do jobs in the kitchen.

6. **Put the incident in the past** - As I am going to use this to learn and become a better person, there is no need for me to keep replaying the situation and wasting my energy. The process is complete and it's time to focus on other things in life.

STEP 4.5- SORRY REALLY DOES SEEM TO BE THE HARDEST WORD

Ok, so the dinner isn't the end of the world and there are far bigger mistakes that we have and will make, but the process of forgiveness is the same, that is, unless you have hurt someone. We are going to call this step 4.5, the apology.

I once heard that apologies are like Brussel sprouts; they are so healthy for us yet leave a bitter taste in our mouth. Saying "I'm sorry" is a real challenge for some. They see it as a sign of weakness, perhaps defeat, it can also make us feel guilty for the mistake we made. Others just hate to admit that they were wrong. For those with low self-esteem, they may feel as if they don't deserve to be forgiven or that the other person may reject their apology, which is enough to put them off apologizing, even when they want to.

It's common for the apology to be left out of the conversation and this makes it almost impossible for the people involved to move forward. This is why I have called it step 4.5, as it is often when we readdress the mistakes that were made and consider other people's feelings, we see the error of our ways. A genuine apology should consist of three elements:

- It shows that you accept responsibility

- It can't contain a 'but' or 'if only'
- There is a way to put things right

Be very careful of the popular 1970s catchphrase "Love means never having to say you're sorry". This sentence should be buried in the 70s where it belongs. We can't use our relationship as an excuse for not needing to apologize for our mistakes. And we certainly can't use it as a reason not to teach our children the importance of sorry. I am reminded of parents towering over their children shouting "say sorry" until the child gives in, knowing it's the only solution. However, forcing someone doesn't mean they have accepted their mistake.

With my children's empty apologies almost hurt more than a lack of apology, in fact, I even say not to say it if they don't mean it or if there is no effort to change the behavior. At the same time, how are they going to learn if I am not brave enough to teach them how to say sorry by apologizing for my mistakes?

When you make your apology, don't feel that you need to make a huge, long speech. We don't want to lose the meaning of the word in a ton of fluff. More often than not, the simplest apology is the most effective. Tell them that you are sorry you hurt them and that you love them.

HOW TO FORGIVE THOSE WHO HURT YOU

"Forgive others, not because they deserve forgiveness, but because you deserve peace."

— **JONATHON LOCKWOOD HUIE**

I have always admired people who have had heinous crimes committed against them, yet they can stand in front of this criminal and forgive them. There is a degree of strength that this requires, an empathy and an incredible ability to understand your emotions.

Jonathan Lockwood Huie really did hit the nail on the head with his quote. Forgiveness isn't about the wrongdoer, it's about the victim. Those that hurt us have to live with what they have done. Some might be genuinely remorseful and offer an apology. It won't change time or undo the action however it is part of their process. Some people are unable to feel any kind of regret or sorrow for what they have done. The same people won't care if you forgive them either. We don't have control over this and waiting for an apology is going to prevent you from moving forward.

YASMIN A.

So, the need to forgive people has to be for your own benefit. It's another action that is rather empowering. Knowing that you have the choice to set yourself free from the pain and leave it in the past. Similarly, when you are holding on to the mistakes others make, they have control over you. And this cannot be. Moving forward towards the new norm means you need to have complete control over your own life. Knowing that by forgiving you can regain your power and set yourself free from anger, makes it easier, especially when you remember that you are doing it for your health, and nobody else.

Knowing that forgiveness is a choice that you can make and then committing to let go of the painful acts are two of the steps that are going to help you to find a new sense of peace. It is not something that you wake up and just do. It might take time, especially when it comes to trust. Having my husband cheat on wasn't an act that I could forgive in the moment. I needed to work at it and at the same time, I needed to learn that he was sorry and that it wasn't going to happen again. When it did happen again, it was time to end this abuse of my trust, my heart, and the complete lack of respect for my boundaries. I never looked back, there were no more opportunities. But I had a choice. I could let them hurt eat away at me, or I could forgive him so that I could find peace.

And forgiving our children? If you don't have children you could be tempted to skip this part, but just in case the future brings you these little bundles of fun, read on!

Little people in our lives are easier to forgive. Our brains easily recognize that they are still learning. Is 10 the magic number or perhaps other moms have a different point in time? There comes a point where in your head you start to think "They should know better by now" and it becomes harder to forgive them. Nevertheless, we have to.

Children, even teenagers look at us as Mum. We don't have emotions we can't be hurt or have any type of problem that could be more serious than theirs. This isn't them being selfish, we just have to remember that they are still learning. And this is an amazing thing! You want your children to continue learning new things, even when they are adults. Forgive your children because it's good for you. Because they are learning how to handle their emotions and that saying sorry is a sign of strength not weakness. Regardless of how hurt you are, go back to step 3 and allow yourself a pause so that you can focus on the needs of your child and keeping the lines of communication open. They need to feel your love not your anger, so step away if you have to and go back when you are calmer. Don't leave it too long because it is very possible that they are hurting, and they could see your pause as punishment.

RELEASING THE PAIN OF GUILT

"Guilt is to the spirit, what pain is to the body."

— ELDER DAVID A. BENDAR

And finally, my friend Guilt. It pops up when you aren't expecting it, can hang around for too long and in some cases, it is just impossible to get rid of. It can also come in all shapes and sizes, sometimes warranted, other times not. More often than not, we are plagued by guilt because of our anger or because of the mistakes we made. There is one type of guilt that needs special attention, and we will call this mother's guilt.

We feel guilty for everything from eating the last chocolate to taking some time for ourselves. We feel guilty for working, for nagging, for not being good enough, you name it. Being a mom is obviously a great responsibility, but I wonder if we underestimate our children.

Going back to my husband, many ask why I didn't leave the first time he was unfaithful. By choosing to leave, I was responsible for breaking up the family home and the thought made me feel immense amounts of guilt. Even just thinking about it made me feel like I would be the worst mom ever, so how would I feel when I actually did it. I would question the effect it would have on my children and they would cope with just one parent. Maybe they would be picked on at school for having a different set up and maybe they would hate me.

What actually happened was nothing. In fact, the biggest drama I had to face was the fight they had over who would get which bedroom in the new house. I made an effort to talk to them about the divorce and encourage them to talk but for them, life went on as normal. Once again, the guilt that had eaten away at me was not necessary. Children are incredibly resilient and much stronger than we give them credit. They also don't seem to analyze decisions as much as we do. It's during this analysis that we tend to start feeling guilty no matter what we decide to do.

As we keep going on our journey to the new you it is necessary to start easing up on the guilt, whether that's mom guilt, survivors' guilt, or any other kind that may rear its ugly head. Tell yourself that you did your best. You ran your fastest, studied the hardest, tried as much as you could. You also need to remember that you know more now than you did in the past, you are wiser now and you can't keep blaming yourself for things you did when you didn't have the same knowledge.

YASMIN A.

Also, while you are replaying situations that you feel guilty about, think about whether you actually had control of the situation. If you can't afford to buy your kids the latest play station, is this really something to beat yourself up over? Are they healthy and happy with what they have? Of course, it would be nice to treat them but there are other things that would be a better way to spend that money.

Make sure that going forward you set clear boundaries. This is a great way to stop feeling guilty about certain things because there are expectations in place. If your parents know that on Sundays you have dinner at home, they will stop asking you to eat with them and so you don't have to feel guilty about saying no. Think about your values and beliefs and start to set boundaries based on them.

Letting go of guilt and learning to forgive yourself and others takes a good sense of self-awareness and in particular those emotions that are associated with these feelings. If you find it hard to sort through the feelings in your mind, I recommend writing about them in a journal. It's such a good way to organize your thoughts and your mind. You will notice that it's easier to see situations in a clearer light and even with a different perspective.

LIVE IN THE PRESENT

As you go about your day, consider how much time you spend thinking about the past and the future. We look back at the decisions we made that have got us to where we are today and wonder if things could have turned out differently. A great deal of time is also spent on the future; planning, saving, working towards our goals. It's unlikely that we are going to just forget our past and we need to feel like we have some control over our future, despite this, we need to learn how to enjoy the moment.

What we can truly rely on in the present. It's the present that we can control - today. You can wake up each morning and decide what you are going to make of that day. You can decide what to do and how to feel. Make the time to sit down, even if it's just for a couple of minutes and enjoy the moment. Feel the sunlight on your face, or the raindrops trickling off your nose. Look around and soak up the beauty of the world, because again, it's your choice to see it.

The new normal might seem like a honeymoon phase. You will probably think that it won't last or that you don't deserve it. Neither of these are true. You have worked hard to make the necessary changes, and this is your reward. That's not to say that you don't need to continue making an effort to benefit from a life of peace instead of anger. Keep writing in your journal as part of the new routine so that you are aware of your emotions and triggers. It is also a great way to monitor which anger management techniques are working for you.

Now is also the perfect time to introduce some new activities to enjoy, and without feeling guilty about doing it. Start putting yourself first every once in a while. Go for a walk because you want to and just be in the moment. Don't worry, putting yourself first sounds like a terribly selfish thing to do, but the next chapter will look at why it's actually quite the opposite.

10

BE COMPASSIONATE TO YOURSELF

We throw the words self-love and self-care around with what I feel is often with little respect for the concepts. For some people, self-love might sound a bit hippy-ish, probably due to its origins in this era. Self-care was also a concept coined in the late 50s but actually comes from medicine. The final chapter is going to be all about looking after yourself, understanding your needs, and appreciating that it is ok to take care of them. To do this, we are going to look at the benefits of self-love, self-care, and self-compassion.

WHAT IS THE DIFFERENCE BETWEEN SELF-LOVE, SELF-CARE, AND SELF-COMPASSION?

The ability to love yourself regardless of anything else and without the need to apologize is known as self-love. It's about accepting yourself and finding gratitude. You respect and even admire yourself. More importantly, it's about putting your physical and mental health before the need to please others.

Self-compassion is recognizing your suffering, your failures, and the things that you don't like about yourself and finding ways to care for yourself even in the difficult times. In the times that we used to punish ourselves for our faults and mistakes, we now need to understand them and find a way to be kind to ourselves. If you are self-compassionate, you know that it's ok not to be perfect. Maybe the hardest part of self-compassion for us is the balance of our emotions, neither suppressing them, nor exaggerating them.

If you ask anyone if they take care of themselves, they will probably say yes although we all know that there is room for improvement. Most of the time, we assume that the question relates to our physical health. In fact, self-care is any activity we intentionally carry out that helps our physical, mental, and emotional health. Self-care is the key to a balanced life. The combination of all three is the key to a happy life.

YOU ARE NOT BEING SELFISH

This is probably one of the most common emotions that arise from the idea of taking care of yourself, in every sense of the word. There is also something more important or more pressing that needs our attention and we will get round to ourselves later on. I laugh because deep down I knew this later on wouldn't occur, but I would still convince myself it would...when everyone else is happy. We also feel that as long as everyone else is happy that we will be too. This is not the case and instead, it can lead us to feel resentment towards our loved ones. Wouldn't it be nice if they could do something nice for us after all we do for them?

The other thing that can happen is that we just burn out. We spend so much time on everyone else that the stress, anxiety, and unhealthy habits catch up with us and we don't have the strength to look after anyone. This is why self-care, -love, and -compassion aren't selfish. It's about taking care of yourself so that you are able to look after others. Being selfish is always thinking about yourself before others, not once in a while.

What we often forget is that we have basic needs and basic rights that we are all entitled to, throughout our entire lives. They don't just stop when we become an adult, get our first job, get married, or become a parent. Even the Declaration of Independence states that we have the right to life, liberty, and the pursuit of happiness. The United Nations has a list of 30 basic human rights. Number 24 is that all humans have the Right to Play, to take a rest from work and relax. So instead of feeling guilty for doing what makes you happy and calm, you need to remind yourself that as an equal family member, you deserve to take time for yourself.

HOW TO START PRACTICING SELF-CARE AND SELF-LOVE

Although not naming it as such, we have already looked at techniques that will improve your self-compassion. Being able to understand your feelings and the triggers behind them promotes empathy. Learning how to forgive and let go of the guilt is also going to help so much. Let's turn our attention to what needs to be done for self-care and self-love.

There are some things that will come up on every self-care list you read. Sleep, eat healthy, balanced diet, drink water, and exercise. Things are common sense but harder to implement if you are already busy. So, the first place is to start saying no to people. Look at each request and decide if it is something you want to do or not. Even just one or two little no's can free up some time that can be dedicated to you. Then, it is a question of starting a new routine which includes these core ideas. Some ideas may include:

- Drink a glass of water with each other drink you have throughout the day.
- Get up 10 minutes earlier so that you can do some exercise, a brisk walk, some yoga, even dancing.
- Don't start out on a massive new diet, just try making small changes. I'm not allowed to eat chocolate unless I have a piece of fruit with it. Try new foods and recipes to see if you can expand your likes to include more nutrients.
- Avoid caffeine before going to bed, replace it with herbal tea, and try deep breathing before falling asleep to relax your mind and body.

Another popular option is mindfulness and meditation, but we will revise this in more detail later on. The following list is quite a long one because I wanted to make sure there were ideas that appeal to everyone. Try the ones that draw your attention, adapt them so that they really motivate you and give you the warm feeling of comfort inside us.

YASMIN A.

Go Green

This isn't related to recycling- which you should also do so that you feel good about helping the planet. I mean the color green. Green is an incredibly positive color. It is the color of balance, harmony, and growth. It can help us to love ourselves more. Visit parks, forests, and green space you can find in nature. If you can't appreciate nature, studies have shown that even looking at pictures of nature can boost your mood. So, you might want to think about getting some new wall decorations or buying a plant or two.

Learn new things

Learning improves your confidence, and it gives you so much more to talk about than the usual "How was your day?" Take the 5 minutes you would spend on social media and look up answers to the questions that have always bugged you. Read as much as you can. Amazingly, just 6 minutes of daily reading can reduce stress by up to 60%. Reading non-fiction can provide a lovely escape from some of our worries and may help you sleep.

Declutter your home

This is one of my favorites. Every once in a while, my kids look at me and say, "She's on one", and they know I'm on a declutter mission. Have a good clean out of wardrobes and cupboards, socks that have no pair, Tupperware with no lids, get rid of it all! A clutter free space can have a great impact on our mental clutter too. Once it's done, not only will you feel like you have been extremely productive, but you will also feel calmer.

Disconnect

Disconnect from technology. Most of us need at least one form of technical device for work, the TV is often on, and the phone is ringing. Basically, there is a constant buzz of electrical waves around us that can't be good. Switch it all off, just for 10 or 15 minutes a day so that your brain gets a break from the screens.

Go to the doctor and the dentist

You have an ache that doesn't seem to shift, or you have put off your checkup with the dentist. Because everyone else is more important you never get round to these things but, you will miss your teeth when you don't have them and getting medical conditions seen to earlier can prevent them from getting worse.

Create a list of your achievements

Just because you haven't won a Nobel Prize or changed the world, it doesn't mean that you haven't got some amazing accomplishments under your belt. Did you finish high school? Have you travelled? Have you got your own home, rented or mortgage? Can you drive? Have you got special skills that have led you to achieve something? What about the smaller things in life? Can you run a mile, complete a Sudoku in 3 minutes or beat any of your personal records?

Spend time with people you want to

It's important to spend time with people who make you feel special, loved and who radiate positivity. Maybe its family or friends or people you haven't been in touch with for a while. If you analyze who you spend your time with and feel like you are lacking people who care about you, respect you and make you feel good, it's time to expand your relationships. You could join a support group, even online support groups to meet people in similar situations. As you start to feel stronger, your advice may even help others.

Get comfortable doing things alone

If you feel like you need somebody to do things it could mean that you are dependent on others for your own happiness. Doing things alone means you don't have to keep to the pace of others, you have more freedom, and you have time to reflect. It's great for your self-esteem and your confidence.

Try to slow down

There are so many things we do because we have to, but we could actually enjoy them if we slowed down. I fly around the supermarket as quickly as I can but if I didn't, I would probably find new ingredients of inspiration for meals. Ironing takes forever, so why not put a film on that you have been meaning to watch. Taking things a little slower enables you to find the positive, simply because there is more time to do it.

Be kind for the sake of being kind

It's perfectly normal to think about doing something and ask, "What's in it for me". We need to do this in order to prioritize our activities and make sure we get everything done. Once a day, try to do something nice for no other reason. Put a silly joke in with your kids' lunch, knock on your neighbor's door and see if they need anything, or help an older person if they need it—just because you can.

Get in touch with your creative side

I genuinely lack creativity and rarely has one of my little craft projects turned out well. Nevertheless, I have great fun trying all these creative hacks that you see online and every once in a while, something turns out ok. You could start off small with a paint by numbers (there are many very intricate paintings you can do now), take some abstract photos to frame and once you are feeling the creative bug, look at ways to renovate old pieces of furniture.

HOW DOES MEDITATION AND MINDFULNESS HELP?

Meditation and mindfulness are mental health tools that create a sense of calmness on the inside and increases are levels of happiness. There are many different kinds and as mentioned before, the theory is simple, but the practice isn't, especially if you are new to either.

Meditation is a form of clearing the mind, a focus on nothing. Mindfulness is the practice of focusing the mind on something. This could be a word, sound, object, smell, or a part of the body. Mindfulness can be sitting, standing, or even walking. It requires slow, deep breaths while focusing on the thing you have chosen. As feelings and concepts enter the mind, we acknowledge them but don't react to them. They float away as we remain focused. Both practices can last for a few minutes or longer, depending on the time that you have. Because they are only short (yet amazingly powerful techniques) it is easier to fit them into your day without making drastic changes.

The other great thing is that you can't go wrong. There is no way that you can hurt yourself or make your situation worse. In fact, by trying, you will only improve as your brain gets better at not letting interferences get in the way.

The benefits of meditation and mindfulness for the physical and mental health have now been well documented, noticeably for stress and anxiety. While we can't take credit for something that has been used for over 2,500 years, healthcare systems like the NHS (the National Health Service in the UK), has recognized mindfulness meditation as good for depression and as many as 30% of GPs refer patients to mindfulness training. Many companies are also now including mindfulness and meditation programs for their employees.

Despite knowing all the benefits, it is easy to give up after the first few attempts. Our brains really struggle with focusing and you might feel like this technique isn't for you. Therefore, I highly recommend getting professional help. This doesn't have to be in the form of therapy. I found joining a yoga class to be greatly beneficial in the early days as instructors can guide you through either practice and you might find it easier to listen to their words. There are also some great apps. Headspace, Calm, and Aura are free and available for Android and iOS. Calm, for example, also has Sleep Stories that can improve your sleep patterns. Try not to give up just yet. Remember, you aren't doing any harm by taking a few minutes to focus the mind and practice deep breathing. You may not notice the benefits straight away, but they will be there. Just think, once you master meditation and/or mindfulness, it will be another thing you can add to your achievements list.

Here are some organizations that provide free mindfulness assistance:

> Mindful.org
> Palousemindfulness.com
> Freemindfulness.org

You might find that if you do start therapy, mindfulness will be used in conjunction with talking therapies. In Chapter 2, we briefly looked at REBT, so let's take a closer look at how this particular type of therapy can increase your self-love and self-care.

HOW CAN RATIONAL EMOTIVE BEHAVIOR THERAPY HELP YOU

REBT works on the theory that the way we think about events causes upset with our emotions and our behaviors and can be a great help when it comes to focusing on the present and more specifically, how we handle unhealthy anger and guilt. Therapists will work with people to identify certain beliefs that are causing them emotional distress, for example rules or expectations that someone has and then use methods to change these ideas into something more realistic or logical.

Rational emotional behavioral therapy works on an ABC model, A is the activity or event, B is the belief about the event, and C is the consequence, or emotional reaction. Traditionally, we would look at our emotions coming from the event, but REBT focuses on our belief of the event. Let's see how this relates to anger.

Anger can lead us to what's known in the trade as irrational core beliefs. When things happen, we can to an extent, turn it into something more dramatic than it really is. A fight with your partner does mean there is no hope or arguing with your kids doesn't mean they don't love you, but this is where the brain may go. REBT doesn't focus on the arguments, but on the belief.

In my personal experience, I found REBT to be a golden ticket when 3 of my loved ones died in a short period of time. My belief was that I had done something to deserve this or that I was destined for a life of suffering. Even reading this now I can see that the idea is irrational but at the time I needed help to see this. On the same topic, I am not a professional therapist, and therefore I am not going to go into the techniques that can help you, it is very individual. However, I do have a worksheet that I used that I think will help you.

If I had to sum up the three self-concepts, I would say that they are three ideas that you not only are entitled to but also deserve. They are about putting yourself first to become a better, stronger person, and ultimately a person who can lead by great examples. They are about making the decision to leap out of the rat race and the turmoil of life and choose to enjoy moments in life that weren't necessarily there yesterday and there is no guarantee that they will be there tomorrow. You have been through some extreme highs and lows and you have suffered for long enough. Learning to love who you are for the good and the bad helps you to see the importance of looking after this self. Our goals are to manage our anger so that we can find peace and happiness and the methods we have looked at will help you to achieve their goals.

If you have found this book informative and useful, I would be incredibly grateful if you could take a few minutes to write an honest review on Amazon for me!

CONCLUSION

It's amazing how sad I feel writing this last chapter—but not to worry, I will process this! I feel sad because despite offering advice and techniques from both research and my own experiences, I want to do more. I want to be able to give you a hug and tell you that you will be ok and that you can survive and find the peace that you are looking for. I want you to see that this is a book based on the heart before science, and that a woman has reached the worst possible place and step by step, she has climbed up. I know that you can do the same.

Reaching the end also makes me feel so grateful to everyone who has read this book. It has reminded me of the importance of writing a journal and if I could give you just one piece of advice from everything that we have seen, it would be to go back to the basics of pen and paper.

CONCLUSION

I started my first journal when I was 10. It was probably a school project or the cool thing to do at that point. Young girls wanted to be able to lock their secrets away. I was 18 when the doctor recommended antidepressants. The placebo effect was apparent and 6 months later I was in therapy. The therapist asked if I kept a journal. By this point I wasn't writing as frequently as I should have been, so I dusted it off and began again.

Some years later, and I have a collection of journals. The latest is just three feet away from me. I admit to apologizing to my journal for abusing it, only writing when I need it instead of the 10-year-old me who would update daily. My journal doesn't care if I write every day, once a month, or once a year. It doesn't judge me for my feelings, and it doesn't tell me what I think I want to hear. It's just there! It's there when I burn the dinner and feel that I have failed. It's there when I mess up in work or shout at my kids before I have looked at all sides of the story. It's there when I need to look back and remember the worst days of my life and it reminds me that there is light at the end of the tunnel. Writing this book has been a little bit like writing in my journal, and for this, I thank you.

Anger hurts, physically and emotionally. Regardless of how bad you are feeling now, there are solutions. If you have read

CONCLUSION

this book it's because you believe this and you have decided to make a change. A huge congratulations to you because you have taken the hardest step. Your body can't cope with so much anger and stress. Neither can your loved ones. If you are a woman who is the victim of anger, though it also seems impossible, some hard decisions have to be made. Try not to think of others when you are making your choice. Children and even parents need to see that you are happy and safe, and they will support your decision and thrive from it.

If you are a man reading this book, then I must also congratulate you and hope that you have learnt more about the differences between the male and female brain. Your loved one, be that partner or family member, is lucky to have a man in their life who is willing to expand their knowledge in order to improve their relationship. As women, we still have this massive stigma about anger, we have no reason to be angry or it's just our hormones making us crazy. The world needs more men like you, those who can move past what society expects of women and actually see us as equals. If you have found this book helpful in seeing things from your loved ones point of view, there will be more books you may find insightful—

And women, despite the differences in brain functions, our rights are the same. Age, gender, religion, disability, wealth,

CONCLUSION

you name it, nothing takes away our right to be happy, or angry.

The key takeaway here is how we deal with that anger. And again, be very careful here. Anger management is not about making our partner happy. It's most certainly not about accepting behavior that you don't deserve. Imagine it's Sunday night and your husband and kids are all asking where their uniforms are. It's not your responsibility to wash, iron, and have everything ready. Anger management isn't about controlling your emotions because people abuse your role. Even if your role is to take care of the home, nobody should assume that all of these jobs are done for them. You can relate the same theory to your colleagues.

If you want to remove a significant amount of your anger quickly, it would be to set your boundaries. I don't want to finish up with more household examples, but they are easily adaptable. Before my anger management, I promise I did try, but people in my house would leave shoes everywhere. In my angry state, I just threw them into the garden, and they all had to go through a shoe hunt. Today, I explain how I feel disrespected when they don't put their shoes where they live, and I have made it easier for them to store their shoes. The attention has moved from the shoes to feeling proud that I don't get angry about it. What surprised me the most,

CONCLUSION

is that when my family heard how much it upset me, they changed their behavior without me having to get angry.

Some people can make changes in a week or two and with something as simple as a reminder to take deep breaths. For others, it can take months and they may need help. Professional help is not the same as it was 20 or even 10 years ago. Choosing help for your anger management isn't a sign of failure or that you are crazy. It's more common than you can imagine, but because of the stigma and the pressure from society, it's not talked about.

My final thought is that this journey should be a positive one for you. I hope you feel a flutter of excitement and motivation. There will be times of hurt as you uncover the triggers of your anger and other emotions. Don't be surprised if things pop up that you hadn't even considered. This is a good thing. You are dusting off the cobwebs of those boxes that contain your buried feelings. To start fresh, we need to learn that it's the burying of feelings that prevents us from moving forward. Don't fear your emotions, even when you are scared of them. Imagine these dark and negative emotions are the key to unlocking this giant iron door that will take you to the happiness you deserve.

Right now, I have an achievement list and a gratitude list to update, not to mention the next book to start planning.

CONCLUSION

Thank you for reading and I would be grateful if you could take a few minutes to leave an honest review on Amazon. The next book will be dedicated to menopause.

REFERENCES

Anger and Trauma. (2014, January 30). Retrieved from https://athealth.com/topics/anger-and-trauma-2/

Are Males and Females Emotionally Equal. (n.d.). Retrieved from https://www.psychologytoday.com/us/blog/good-thinking/201406/are-males-and-females-equally-emotional

Buczynski, R. (2020a, August 28). How Anger Affects the Brain and Body [Infographic]. Retrieved from https://www.nicabm.com/how-anger-affects-the-brain-and-body-infographic/

Buczynski, R. (2020b, August 28). How Anger Affects the Brain and Body [Infographic]. Retrieved from https://www.nicabm.com/how-anger-affects-the-brain-and-body-infographic/

REFERENCES

Burgess, L. (2017, October 7). Eight benefits of crying: Why it's good to shed a few tears. Retrieved from https://www.medicalnewstoday.com/articles/319631

Farr, N. (2020, April 2). Now More Than Ever: Books, Books, Books! Retrieved from https://greatist.com/connect/why-reading-is-essential#1

Feldman, D. B. (2017, July 7). Why the Five Stages of Grief Are Wrong. Retrieved from https://www.psychologytoday.com/us/blog/supersurvivors/201707/why-the-five-stages-grief-are-wrong

Gallego, R. (2019, June 10). Child-to-parent Violence and Parent-to-child Violence: A Meta-analytic Review. Retrieved from https://journals.copmadrid.org/ejpalc/art/ejpalc2019a4

Golden, B. (2016, September 17). What Constitutes "Healthy Anger"? Retrieved from https://www.psychologytoday.com/us/blog/overcoming-destructive-anger/201608/what-constitutes-healthy-anger

Gunther, R. (2019, September 30). How Anger Affects Intimate Relationships. Retrieved from https://www.psychologytoday.com/us/blog/rediscovering-love/201908/how-anger-affects-intimate-relationships

Haley, E. (2020, April 16). Types of Grief: Yes, there's more than one. Retrieved from https://whatsyourgrief.com/types-of-grief/

Hanson, R. (2020, June 18). The Science of Positive Brain Change. Retrieved from https://www.rickhanson.net/the-science-of-positive-brain-change/

Hansson, M. (2017, December 1). NHS recognition of mindfulness meditation is good for depression | Mia Hansson. Retrieved from https://www.theguardian.com/society/2013/feb/26/mindfulness-meditation-depression-nhs

History-of-EQ. (2017, November 24). Retrieved from https://www.emotionalintelligencecourse.com/history-of-eq/

Holler, M. (2019, June 17). Pregnancy, Parenting, Lifestyle, Beauty: Tips & Advice | mom.com. Retrieved from https://mom.com/momlife/signs-of-a-healthy-brain/you-have-good-friends

May, C. (2017, August 30). Are Women More Emotionally Expressive Than Men? Retrieved from https://www.scientificamerican.com/article/are-women-more-emotionally-expressive-than-men/

Mayo Clinic. (2020, April 18). Relaxation techniques: Try these steps to reduce stress. Retrieved from https://www.

mayoclinic.org/healthy-lifestyle/stress-management/in-depth/relaxation-technique/art-20045368?reDate=31102020

NHS. (2020, October 8). Psychological therapies for stress, anxiety and depression. Retrieved from https://www.nhs.uk/conditions/cognitive-behavioral-therapy-cbt/

Plataforma SINC. (2010, June 1). What happens when we get angry? Retrieved from https://www.sciencedaily.com/releases/2010/05/100531082603.htm#:%7E:text=Summary%3A,the%20brain%20becomes%20more%20stimulated

Rational Emotive Behavior Therapy. (n.d.). Retrieved from https://www.psychologytoday.com/intl/therapy-types/rational-emotive-behavior-therapy

Self-harm and teenagers. (2019, February 4). Retrieved from https://raisingchildren.net.au/teens/mental-health-physical-health/mental-health-disorders-concerns/self-harm

Stromberg, J. (2014, September 24). 7 things marshmallows teach us about self-control. Retrieved from https://www.vox.com/2014/9/24/6833469/marshmallow-test-self-control

REFERENCES

The Cycle of Anger (Worksheet). (n.d.). Retrieved from https://www.therapistaid.com/therapy-worksheet/cycle-of-anger

Types of Trauma. (2020, August 25). Retrieved from http://teachtrauma.com/information-about-trauma/types-of-trauma/

WebMD. (2000, January 1). Men and Anger Management. Retrieved from https://www.webmd.com/men/guide/anger-management#1

Wikipedia contributors. (2020, October 13). Anger management. Retrieved from https://en.wikipedia.org/wiki/Anger_management

Wiley, C. (2020, October 19). Is There Such a Thing as Healthy Anger? Retrieved from https://www.talkspace.com/blog/healthy-anger-what-is-definition-guide/

www.ingramcontent.com/pod-product-compliance
Lightning Source LLC
Chambersburg PA
CBHW062052280426
43661CB00088B/731